OVERVIEW

This work is largely inspired by reading works of Hon'ble Justice Krishna Iyer. He was of the opinion that a person has the right to bail if there is a possibility that such release shall not make the trial suffer and that only a convicted criminal should be kept in prison.

In my limited practice I have seen people spend month's in prison on mere accusation and the quantity is so huge that it takes months for bail applications to be heard in regular course. I have seen people suffer due to this regressive system and I believe that after two centuries its about time we bring change in the approach of criminal justice system in this country. The current system was to aid the so called rulers to rule over the mass and hence it was punitive in nature so they can instill fear in masses and get away with it but it is no more the case. It has been 73 years of independence and yet the criminal justice system remains the same. So this book suggests for replacing the punitive system with a reformative system highlighting that the prisoners are human too and citizen of this country too having similar rights as that of anyone else unless explicitly barred by law.

I would want to thank my senior Adv. Khurshid Alam Sir for his continuous guidance during this book and to my friends and family who were always

up for a good debate on the ideas I
wanted to put in here.

INDEX

Chapter- 1 Understanding the Macaulay Syndrome

In words of Justice V.R. Krishna Iyer the Indian Penal System suffers from the Macaulay Syndrome. To make it convenient for people, Thomas Babington Macaulay is the person responsible for the Indian Penal Code for what it is. He was the chairman of the 1834 Law Commission and despite a second law commission, the present Indian Penal Code enacted in 1860 is considered single handed work of Macaulay and this is the beginning of the problem that the current sentencing policy suffers; it's so ancient that in some areas do not fit well in today's modern age society. Macaulay had complete independence in drafting the new unified penal law of the country and hence without any proper debate and discussion the laws were being formulated for a country. The same can be acceptable for the period of colonial era but the fact that to this day the same law which was enacted by a colonial official is still in existence in the country is kind of absurd in itself. Macaulay was a fan of punishing the offender for the crime he's committed and as his supporters consider his fanaticism for punishment is clear in his "baby". Macaulay said 'We must grant impunity to the vast majority of those omissions which a benevolent morality would pronounce reprehensible, and must content ourselves with punishing such omissions only when they are distinguished from the rest by some circumstance which marks them out as peculiarly fit objects of penal legislation'[1] but his penal policies are starkly different from what has been said about him by his native land authors. The punitive measures adopted in the sentencing process is

---

[1] Macaulay on Adam Smith and liability for omissions, see Knud Haakonssen, *"The Science of the Legislator"* (Cambridge University Press, 1981)

barbaric if nothing worse when you look at it in the first glance itself.

It is crucial to know that much of the Draft Penal Code (later enacted as Indian Penal Code in 1860) was formulated in a manner to assist the governance of the East India Company in the territory as only 5 of the 26 chapters concern themselves with offences against an individual and the rest are for offences against the state or in words of Adam Smith 'laws of police'[2] and not 'laws of justice'. Macaulay's way was to assist the authoritarian colonial rule as it is mentioned that he wanted the draft penal code to be written in such a manner which can be easily interpreted, hence free of the legal jargons and also wanted to take away the freedom of judiciary be trying to make the code such that nothing is left for judicial interpretation.[3] It is

---

[2] Adam Smith, *Lectures on Jurisprudence*, ed. R. L. Meek, D. D. Raphael and P. G. Stein, vol. V of the Glasgow Edition of the Works and Correspondence of Adam Smith (Indianapolis: Liberty Fund, 1982). Accessed from http://oll.libertyfund.org/title/196/55636/920225 on 01-05-2020

clear that as the penal code was drafted in the colonial era by an official appointed by the colonial government to form a legislature to bring all forms of criminal activities under one act for the entire territory under control of the colonial government that such law shall be heavily influenced by the laws on crimes in the Great Britain and for the most part to provide ease to the East India to conduct operations. Briefly, the code came as solution by replacing a patchwork of Muslim and Hindu laws covered in the garb of existing English laws in the Great Britain and East Indian Company regulations.

Macaulay's intent can be found in his quote while referring to the Draft Penal Code as he said, "We must at present do our best to form a class who may be interpreters between us

---

[3] Bibek Debroy, *Learning from Macaulay*, The Week Magazine, December 28, 2019 Accessed from https://www.theweek.in/columns/bibek-debroy/2019/12/28/learning-from-macaulay.html on 27-06-2020

and the millions whom we govern, a class of persons Indian in blood and colour, but English in tastes, in opinions, in morals and in intellect. To that class we may leave it to refine the vernacular dialects with terms of science borrowed from the Western nomenclature, and to render them by degrees fit vehicles for conveying knowledge to the great mass of the population."[4] This tells that the law should be such that people who are "like-minded" shall help it reach the common Indian as Indian's in general weren't of "English Taste" and hence that there was intent to maintain English Law relevant in this part of the world and so did the people responsible for making the laws in the post-Independence era and keeping the 'LEGACY' of Macaulay alive to this date.

---

[4] Bibek Debroy, *The Macaulay We Don't Know*, The Indian Express on Thursday, October 15, 2020, Accessed at https://indianexpress.com/article/opinion/columns/the-macaulay-we-dont-know-ipc-macaulay-indian-penal-code-law-commission-4831988/

It is that my personal opinion is such that State is a part of the society and in an aim of attaining a crime-free society we cannot permit the state to commit crimes because inflicting pain on criminals is criminal in nature in itself and hence every time a State Agency sentences a person it commits a crime because this is the country of Gandhi whose visions is so immaculately incorporated in the Constitution of India and not of Macaulay who saw "Indian blood and colour" people as different to his kind. To Gandhi every criminal was a patient[5] and that prison was to be a hospital for such patients where they could be treated and be released when fit. Unfortunately Gandhi didn't live long enough to bring an end to the sentencing laws in the country but I believe even he wouldn't have wanted for people who brought an end to his life to undergo sentencing

---

[5] Justice V. R. Krishna Iyer, *Law, Lawyer and Justice*, Published by D.K. Publishers (1985), pg. 8

in the manner they did under this brutish penal code. From Socrates, thro' Jesus to Gandhi, the extraordinary saints have told the world that the wrongdoing of taking punitive measures against individual, tho' perpetrated by the State, is wrongdoing in no way different. It is essential to understand that the current law focuses on punishing the person for the crime he has committed and not for his character reformation to outgrow the cause that led to him committing the crime in the first place. Justice V. R. Krishna Iyer addressing a student group at Indian Law Institute, Delhi called people who believe the violence of law and the indignity of humiliation are the only potent weapons as people suffering from the 'Macaulay Syndrome' and addresses such group of people as 'Criminological Morons' and rightly so.

The current penal law is in contradiction to the Constitution on many constituents which it lists as offences under the law and one such classic example is the authoritarian use of Blasphemy and Sedition content which exists despite Freedom of Speech being a fundamental right and still showing disaffection is considered crime?[6] But yet those in power use these laws often to curb opposing forces of their fundamental right making a tedious task for the courts to create a balance between the draconian penal law that exists in the country and the Constitution which is the law of the land while interpreting on case to case basis. Justice Deepak Gupta as recent as in 2019 also stated that the law of sedition in India needs to be toned down if not abolished completely and that any attempt to stifle criticism will

---

[6] Nitin Pai, *Macaulay's IPC was radical in 19th Century. Now, shift power balance toward Indian Citizens*, The Print, 22nd October 2019 Accessed on 10.10.2020 at https://theprint.in/opinion/macaulay-ipc-radical-in-19th-century-time-to-shift-power-balance-towards-indians/309374/

turn India into "a police state"[7] taking us back to Adam Smith's "law of police" theory. An excerpt from the Justice Deepak Gupta lecture is *"Whether it be Buddha, Mahavira, Jesus Christ, Prophet Mohammad, Guru Nanak Dev, Martin Luther, Kabir, Raja Ram Mohan Roy, Swami Dayanand Saraswati, Karl Marx or Mahatma Gandhi, new thoughts and religious practices would not have been established if they had quietly to the views of their forefathers and had not questioned the existing religious practices, beliefs and rituals."* It should also be noted that post-Independence when it was thought that sedition shall be construed constitutionally invalid, Justice Sarjoo Prasad, then Judge at High Court of Judicature at Patna, Bihar in a case observed in the following manner

---

[7] Justice Deepak Gupta, 7th September 2019, Lectures organized by Praleen Public Charitable Trust and Lecture Committee in Ahmedabad, Accessed on 08.06.2020 at https://thewire.in/law/justice-deepak-gupta-supreme-court-sedition

""I am compelled to observe that from the above discussions of the Supreme Court judgments, it follows logically that if a person were to go on inciting murder or other cognizable offences either through the press or by word of mouth, he would be free to do so with impunity inasmuch as he would claim the privilege of exercising his fundamental right of freedom of speech and expression. Any legislation which seeks or would seek to curb this right of the person concerned would not be saved under article 19 (2) of the Constitution and would have to be declared void. This would be so, because such speech or expression on the part of the individual would fall neither under libel nor slander nor defamation nor contempt of court nor any matter which of- fends against decency or morality or which undermines the security of or tends to overthrow the State. I cannot with equanimity contemplate such an anomalous situation but the conclusion appears to be unavoidable on the authority of the Supreme Court judgments with which we are bound. I, there- fore, wish that my decision on the point would sooner than ever come to be tested by the Supreme Court itself and the position reexamined in the light of the anomalous situation pointed out above. It seems to me that the words used in the Constitution Act should be assigned a wide and liberal connotation even though they occur in a clause which pro- vides an exception to the fundamental right vouchsafed under article 19 (1)(a) of the Constitution Act."[8]

This observation was relied from Romesh Thappar's case[9] but was later set aside by the Supreme Court in 1952 which called for the first amendment to the Constitution. The

---

[8] The State of Bihar Vs. Shailabala Devi, 1952 AIR 329
[9] Romesh Thappar Vs. The State of Madras, 1950 AIR 124

Court has had to time and again define what should amount to sedition and how the law should be used in Kedar Nath[10], by referring to the same in Bilal Ahmed Kaloo's[11] case. It should also be brought to notice that at the time the Supreme Court formulated the guidelines for sedition laws, it was still a non-cognisable offence but it was in 1974 that the lawmakers of the country decided to make it a cognizable offence hence making the law worse considering it was being done for the citizens of a free country and yet seemed like a law being made by an insecure group of people who couldn't handle criticism. Since then, this has been misused at will by the government agencies and particularly political forces with the aid of police forces. There have been various instances, a good majority of the total number of cases filed under the law of

[10] Kedar Nath Singh Vs. State of Bihar, 1962 AIR 955
[11] Bilal Ahmed Kaloo Vs. State of Andhra Pradesh, Crl. Apl. No. 81/97 SC

sedition, wherein the final verdict says that the person accused of committing the crime had not committed the crime of sedition according to guidelines held by the constitutional bench in Kedar Nath[12] case and that in 2015, the Bombay High Court had to make a suggestion in one it's judgments[13] that police officials should make an effort to take the opinion of their superior officers before making an arrest for sedition, directing towards that police official's misuse of the provided weapon.

Another problem with this code is that it does not consider all citizens equal even in the chapter where it covers offences against individuals as there are many laws which are sex specific for example the definition of Rape in Indian Penal Code is such that when read it construes that only a man can be the Culprit and that

---

[12] Ibid, pg. 5
[13] Sanskar Marathe Vs. The State of Maharashtra, Bom Cri.PIL 3/2015 (21) 17/03/2015

only a woman can be a victim and such was also the conditions of Adultery law which was recently abolished by the Supreme Court[14] was also such that it meant no woman could commit the offence of adultery and that is was just men who could commit the crime. The Apex Court rightly held it unconstitutional.

Another instance where the Apex Court had to intervene and hold a content of the Penal Code unconstitutional recently was the issue of Section 377 which was the reason behind homosexuality been considered as a criminal offence in the Country. Something which is so personal for a human, his personal sexual orientation was administered by state in 21st Century India until the Supreme Court finally settled it after dismissing a judgment of Delhi High Court[15] which had

---

[14] Joseph Shine Vs. Union of India, 2018 SCC OnLine SC 1676
[15] Naz Foundation Vs. Government of NCT of Delhi, 2010 CriLJ 94 (Del)

decriminalized Homosexuality and suggested to scrap the section out of Indian Penal System almost a decade before Supreme Court. Before the Supreme Court had decriminalized homosexuality[16] and after it had revoked the Delhi High Court judgment[17], a book compiling of Justice Leila Seth[18] was published in which she had advocated for many reforms in the legal system as a whole like mentioning the Uniform Civil Code to include people from all religious backgrounds so as to safeguard the interest of women belonging to minority religious sects but the highlight was the chapter titled "You're Criminal if Gay". Mother of notable writer Vikram Seth, who happens to be openly gay, then at 84 said India needs to follow the rights

---

[16] Navtej Singh Johar & Ors. Vs. Union of India, SC Writ Petition (Criminal) No. 76 of 2016

[17] Suresh Kumar Kaushal & Anr. Vs, Naz Foundation and Ors., MANU/SC/1278/2013

[18] Leila Seth, *Talking of Justice: People's Rights in Modern India*, Published by Aleph Book Company, 2014

based vision while formulating the laws from the Constitution, while the lawmakers of the country try formulating the laws by looking at the chart of offences and their punishment provided in the Penal Code. It took so long for the State to understand that they have no business in the bedroom of an individual tells how authoritarian and state-controlling the draft penal code is.

Much in the similar light of sedition laws, another act was passed by the Indira Gandhi-led government in year 1980 named as 'National Security Act' which allowed for preventive detention by the authorities in the name of National Security. The number of detainees under this law was said to be at 14,57,779, that is more than 1.45 Million people as per the 177th Law Commission Report of 2001. This is a weapon so frequently used by the government agencies as it allows them to put anyone behind bars without giving anyone any explanation for the same and that the person is kept under arrest without being provided the chance to be heard, which in itself is in violation of Principles of Natural Justice but guess this law does not fall in the basket of the same but in the basket of laws made by the post-colonial era rulers to rule their masses with ease. An internal review of habeas corpus held by South Asian Human Rights Documentation (SAHRDC) demonstrated that the police frequently depend on the NSA when they are reluctant or incapable to make a suitable criminal case under the Constitution and legal law. It found that there is a standard example of utilizing preventive confinement, for example, to address the current exercises of recidivists and organized crime; to sidestep a trial when witnesses were reluctant to affirm; and to forestall discharge on bail. Basically, the police appear to consistently utilize preventive confinement in more troublesome criminal law situations when shortcoming or idiocy may make law authorization troublesome.[19] The history of this act can be traced back also to the colonial era as the first act enabling authorities to detain individuals in the name of public order without any trial. The act was named Bengal Regulation III and it was enacted in the year 1818 with the sole intention to arrest individuals in the name of defense and public order by the East India Company officials. The Rowlatt Act of 1919 was a subsequent piece of legislature to the former Bengal Regulation III which allowed the monster in Dyer (a personality like his does not deserve to be remembered for any sort of

---

[19] Ravi Nair, *National Security Act: Obscuring the Flaws in India's Criminal Justice System*, Published by The Wire on 05/03/2018 Accessed at https://thewire.in/caste/national-security-act-obscuring-flaws-indias-criminal-justice-system

military honour) to walk free after what he did in Jallianwalah Bagh, the structure that still haunts visitors of what the people on that morning would have gone through. The law was such that Winston Churchill, then the British Secretary of War called the massacre as "a monstrous event.... Without precedent or parallel in the modern history of empire" and insisted that it was Dyer who was evil and not the empire but I say it was the policy makers and the existing legal system that was evil that allowed a man to walk scot-free despite committing such a heinous crime. Even the sufferers of the Rowlatt Act when came in a position to draft laws for the new independent India were the first to pass a law for preventive detention in 1950 itself, a move that looked like a particular group of people thought of themselves in a position enjoyed by colonial officials in pre-independent India and a sense of retaining that authoritative control over mass can be found from the piece of legislature, which was discussed in detail in A. K. Gopalan[20] case wherein the reasoning that came out that the Fundamental Rights were in silos in themselves and were not interconnected, and constituted independent articles so it tells so much about sudden shift of power and assumption by Indian people who were "English in Taste" that they were now the new British of the country and that it was in their hands to "administrate" the mass in the righteous manner and that such laws were required tools for the same. If in today's modern society, the state can arrest any individual without having to answer to any authority without releasing any detail pertaining to the arrest in public domain if it so wishes to, then this should not be preventive detention but illegal confinement

---

[20] A.K. Gopalan Vs. State of Madras, AIR 1950 SC 27

committed by the state. There is absolutely no logical reason behind hiding the details pertaining to the arrest and just mentioning the ground to be to ensure public order and safety and be free to arrest any individual. This should make every individual uncomfortable because tomorrow anyone could be arrested because the police just 'felt like' it and worst part is that they won't be questioned for the wrongful act committed by wrongful officials on the wish of on most occasion a wrongful person who happens to have some sort of influence over the government. It is important here to mention the instance where Mahatma Gandhi wrote a letter to the press expressing his dissatisfaction to the Rowlatt Acts of 1919 which reads as, "Secret violence is confined to isolated and very small parts of India and to a microscopic body of the people. But the passing of the Bills designed to affect the whole of India and its people and arming the government with power out of all proportion to the situation sought to be dealt with, is a greater danger."[21] And as mentioned above, Gandhi unfortunately didn't live long enough to bring an end to the draconian penal system in India. He didn't envision prisons as trauma centers nor did he see a place for things like preventive detention in a free India but as it happens to be, these things well exist while we continue calling Gandhi the father of the nation.

The worst the state can do is be fearful of opposing voices and put them under arrest without being answerable? Not in the Indian Legal System. The penal laws in India to this day are so authoritative and so barbaric that preventive detention happens to sit outside the worst set of laws but its gross misuse makes it a

---

[21] M.K. Gandhi, *Selected Letters of Mahatma Gandhi*, ed. by Shriman Narayan, Published by Navajivan Publishing House Ahmedabad

standout. Most recently there was detention done under NSA against 3 men in Bulandshahr district of Uttar Pradesh as they were being accused for cow slaughter. This resulted in a communal mob violence in which a police constable succumbed to death and following the death the 3 men were arrested under NSA and not anyone from the mob which shows the absolute misuse of the Act. On numerous accounts journalists have been arrested and notable individuals working or speaking against those in government or their will have to undergo such arrests under various acts allowing for the immediate arrest of the person they want to be behind the bars and under custody.

Finally talks pertaining to proper restructuring of the Indian Penal Code have begun in the corridors of Central Government as on October 20, 2019. A senior government official was quoted as saying "the Code requires major revisions because the idea behind the overhaul is that the master-servant concept envisaged in [the] IPC should change"[22] and the same has been mentioned from various public platforms since. It is nice to see that the intent is now there to bring an end to the 160 year old law which should've lasted half that time at best if the members of the first law making body would have decided to push for a citizen-centric law instead of the current state-centric laws. Funny how they revolted against the same authoritarian system and then lobby-d together to keep the same cruel penal law for them to now use themselves against the common mass and hence putting themselves in the position enjoyed by the British officials before the country got independent from them.

[22] Tariq Ahmad, *India: Government Begins Discussions on Overhauling Colonial-Era Penal Code*, Library of Congress, December 9, 2019 Accessed from https://www.loc.gov/law/foreign-news/article/india-government-begins-discussions-on-overhauling-colonial-era-penal-code/ on 07.07.2020

There has been a spark rise in the cases of mob-lynching cases that have found themselves in the limelight of the media ever since Mr. Narendra Modi-led BJP formed government at centre in 2014 from various parts of the country and most of them being caused from communal incitement (or is shown so before proper investigation result differs while conducting the media trial in studios) and the victims of this crime are brutally injured, tortured and often murdered. This rise has caused a nationwide outcry for a separate law for mob-lynching and it was this outcry that led to this government considering the restructuring of the Indian Penal Code (IPC), 1860. When cornered in the Rajya Sabha during the Question Hour to opposition leaders questions on government's actions on curbing the mob-lynching activities in the country, Mr. Amit Shah, the Minister for Home Affairs responded by saying, "Under the Bureau of Police Research and Development (BPR&D), a committee has been set up to make changes in the IPC and Cr.P.C. We will start working on amendments after receiving recommendations from the committee"[23] and that the government while making the amendments shall consider various suggestions made by the apex court in its various judgments over the period of 69-70 years. While making a speech in August, 2019 at 49th Foundation day of Bureau of Police Research and Development he also emphasized that the organization should come up in a leadership role by spearheading a nationwide research to make changes to the penal policies/laws in India.

There is a strong reason for the restructuring of the penal laws in the

---

[23] The Economic Times, December 04,2019, Accessed from https://economictimes.indiatimes.com/news/politics-and-nation/committee-to-suggest-necessary-amendments-in-ipc-crpc-to-curb-mob-lynching/articleshow/72364528.cms on 07.07.2020

country and to make them more citizen-centric because in the current structure where the laws are state-centric, the government uses these laws in testing times to play with the emotion of the masses. Like for example new guidelines are formulated every time a rape case gets nationwide interest and the laws become more stringent and stringent every time and this is because for two reasons, first being that the government wishes to bail itself by getting the support of the people who are always demanding for stricter punishments and secondly to protect themselves from the backlash of the same group of people. But has this approach worked? This is because these amendments are often brought in a rush to win on the public sentiments and hence lack basic research and hence increases the liability on the judicial system to strike the balance. A law being made stricter might bring pleasure to the society to see something has been done to decrease the possibility of the crime being repeated in future but has a tumbling effect on the criminal justice system.

One of the lesser discussed provisions of law outside the people belonging to legal fraternity circle is the offence of Contempt which had hit the highlights in the country in the Prashant Bhushan[24] case wherein the apex court had taken cognizance on a suo-motu basis over his remarks in particular in a 2009 interview where he had made certain allegations against former Chief Justice's of India passing degrading comments on them among other incidents put together, each relating to his comments on the apex court and the judicial system. Contempt of Court was also an English law which remained in England where it originated until 10

---

[24] Prashant Bhushan And Anr., Suo Motu Contempt Petition (CRL) No. 1 of 2020

December, 2012. The Law Commission presented a report on 4th December and the same was debated in the House of Lords on 10th, and accepted and passed on the same day but it so happens to stay in existence in its once colony, India. The country that gave the law understood it has no space in the modern society but somehow the country that took it still happens to hold on to it. It's like how Mr. Ratan Tata himself loves to drive around in a Honda but people still want to buy a Tata. In words of Justice Deepak Gupta, "We all must be open to criticism. The judiciary is not above criticism. If judges of the superior courts were to take note of all the contemptuous communications received by them, there would be no work other than the contempt proceedings. In fact I welcome criticism of the judiciary because only if there is criticism, will there be improvement. Not only should there be criticism but there must be introspection. When we introspect, we will find that many decisions taken by us need to be corrected. Criticism of the executive, the judiciary, the bureaucracy or the armed forces cannot be termed sedition. In case we attempt to stifle criticism of the institutions – whether it be the legislature, the executive or the judiciary or other bodies of the state – we shall become a police state instead of a democracy and this the founding fathers never expected this country to be". He concluded his address by saying that if this country is to progress beyond the field of commerce and industry to human rights and set an example by being a successful democracy and not just the largest then the voice of the people can never be stifled and hence what happened in Prashant Bhushan case exposed the fallacy of the existing penal system as the court in my opinion did observe that according to the provisions of penal law the person did commit a crime and hence must be punished as the current penal laws is all about punishing the offender for the crime he has so committed and nothing else but the court was also convinced that such criticism should not affect the court and hence the Re.1 fine was as I saw the entire judicial system's coming together and mocking the penal system existing in the country as they didn't acquit him of the offence neither punished him as they would have pleased to and the Re.1 punishment was laugh at the penal policies.

The criminal law is one of the most crucial connection which characterizes the connection between a state and its residents. Subsequently, it is desirable if this relationship is characterized correctly and plainly in the punitive resolutions. The criminal law which is viewed as the most strong State instrument confining person's major right to life and individual freedom must be liberated from irregularities and ambiguities. In any case, of late dubiousness and equivocalness seems, by all accounts, to be the direct principle of the current day administrative mediations. The three previously mentioned characteristics of a decent code which Macaulay esteemed have been given back by with regards to administrative drafting. The equivocal style utilized in criminal laws mirror their need for accuracy. Evident irregularities in criminal laws of India make it hard for common residents and even legitimate specialists to comprehend the extent of a specific arrangement. From one viewpoint, IPC and its alterations keep on being dependent upon steady legal translation verging law-production because of moderate advancement in law changes. While, then again, the governing body and the leader keeps on dozing on urgent law change proposals made by master bodies and advisory groups. In this manner, the IPC and its ongoing enemy of assault revisions keep on sickly from ambiguities, irregularities, and administrative disregard towards its reconstruction. A hurried enactment, drafted with an aim to quiet open motivation, may forecast well for optics and political manner of speaking. Be that as it may, in the knowing the past it bargains the nature of law changes, and stops up the legal framework with petitions appealing to God for a definitive announcement on the law. The Parliament which might have acquired fundamental changes the IPC, left immaculate by 2013 alteration Act, has botched one more chance. By bringing shallow changes, the State seems to have washed its hands, from tending to the additionally squeezing requirement for an extensive amendment of the reformatory code. Also, the State account of prevention is only a confused institutional animosity, confined from ground real factors. What is normal from any administration isn't simple entry of laws yet to direct careful examination, evaluate its discoveries and apply reason under the steady gaze of making any law. Without an all encompassing examination situated methodology, the council will keep on passing equivocal and omnibus laws which dismisses cardinal standards of criminal law, and established qualities. It serves well to all partners in a criminal equity framework to endure as a top priority that regard and adherence to laws must be accomplished when the administrators perceives the need of accommodating individual rights with that of society, along with the State enthusiasm for keeping up law and order.

This Penal System was made for the Indians in 1830's and not for the Indians in 2030's and hence the work to scrap it should begin from the 2020's! The current penal law is inefficient as the same is ancient, obsolete, barbaric, state-centric and focuses on punishment as the sole course towards reducing recidivism amongst individuals and these are the reasons why a complete restructuring of the IPC, Cr.P.C. and other penal laws need to be reformed starting from these two as they are the foundation for penal laws in the country.

Chapter 2: Indian Penal Law- For the State, By the State, Of the State

The constituent assembly drafted a Constitution which they called would be the law of the land and that all the laws in the country should be derived from this Constitution and that any law contrary to the Constitution shall be held invalid being unconstitutional in nature. The same assembly members added that it is a democratic state wherein the government shall be for the people, by the people and of the people. Simultaneously they were allowing penal laws to be for the State, by the State and of the State. When I say this, what I mean is, that the penal law is of the nature that it is to protect the state against individuals more than it is to protect the individual to enjoy his basic rights.

Any colonial legislation had to be authoritarian when it dealt with penal policies because the same was brought to aid the East India Company and protect its officials so that they could control the masses and hence in their list of offences a lot many offences were offences against the state and not offences against the individual. When the priority is protection of state and not of the individual it is often misused by the same people it is meant to protect by enabling them to use these protective measures to exploit their position to have an unlawful advantage over an individual being on the receiving end of the same. We hear about penal policies to be made more stringent, but the same should be for everyone? If a company is considered as an individual for all legal purposes and is represented by its directors then why the State can't be treated as an individual too and its concerned authority are summoned to represent the State? And that similar measure is taken against both such representatives. Recently, the Bombay Stock Exchange crash of 1992 story is doing rounds as multiple web series and movies are being made on the scapegoat Mr. Harshad Mehta showcasing his story from different perspectives but what is essential here is that the man was dead after being diagnosed with a disease in prison because the crime he committed was finding a default in the regulation bank policies and exploited his position. Similarly, during the UPA – led government Mr. A. Raja was accused of the 2g Spectrum Scandal. What happened to the State agency which was responsible of allocating spectrum and which allocated the same on allegedly preferential basis. The treatment of the two accused was vividly present in front of the entire country to see when in 2017 A. Raja along with all other accused in 2g Spectrum Scam were acquitted

It's not completely the fault of the constituent assembly that was responsible for drafting the Constitution and giving this country the law that it would eventually be governed with, but the problem has remained with the legal officers and experts relying on Salmond's jurisprudence to interpret the law. Salmond is considered as the all in all authority over any legal idea by Indian Law students and practitioners all along and the same is taught in the institutions as well. Salmond distincts Criminal law from Civil Law by saying that while the latter is termed as "private wrongs", the former is classified as "public wrongs".[25] Now any activity against the state is criminal in nature and it should be but then the definition of

---

[25] P. J. Fitzgerald, *Salmond on Jurisprudence*, 12th Edition, Published by Sweet & Maxwell (2020) pg. 91

State needs to be altered and when protecting the state under penal laws, the definition should not be taken out of Article 12 of the Constitution and if the protection is granted to everyone falling under that definition of State, then other parts of the penal law should also be in light of the Constitution. India is not a colonial state anymore where the officials need to be safeguarded in the manner they were needed to during the colonial era. India suffers from the Colonial hangover as the manner in which Law Enforcement Agencies function in the country to this day is in a lot of ways similar to how the colonial officials did. When an individual finds a person in uniform around him, he feels more fear than feeling safe, the presence of police does not give him the feeling of security but rather adds to his stress that the police might unnecessarily trouble him. This behaviour is not stopped and continues to stay and shine in the Indian Society. We the people of the country still fear the Khakee like our ancestors used to while they saw the officials of Crown Representative Police (present day Central Reserve Police Force, CRPF) and other such forces employed by the East India Company to help the rule and regulate the territory. This is because the individual is aware that there is an entire pool of legislations that the state can use against him despite him not actually doing anything wrong and that the process to prove himself innocent can be long and a tedious one and hence people wish to maintain a "SAFE" distance from the State and its agents.

The most important change brought in the Amendment to Cr.P.C. in year 1973 was that the State for the first time declared that from thereon the purpose of penal law shall be to reform an individual and not mere punishment for the offence he has so committed. This was a noble idea, which from my perspective remained only an idea which to date is yet to be achieved in its true sense. I am not saying that there has been no development in this direction ever since but not significant much.

The Juvenile Justice Act is an exemplary example of reformative law and also the text to what it is today to what it was first when the Whipping Act of 1864 was passed which dealt with crimes committed by juveniles which allowed the officials to whip the offenders for their crimes. So, in simpler words, the people who drafted our current penal laws believed in whipping children for crimes committed. This tells us their purpose of enacting penal laws. This act is actually written in such a manner which ensures that the rehabilitation of the child is prioritized and that he is protected from unnecessary punitive measures otherwise taken in a general prison. The Section 45 of the Act reads : "The state government is empowered to ensure effective linkages between various governmental, non – governmental, corporate and other community agencies for the sake of rehabilitation and social integration of the child." But just like any opportunity to play on the people's sentiments when it was found that one of the accused in the infamous Delhi Rape Case of 2012 was a juvenile at the time of committing the crime and hence was to be treated like one despite it was alleged that he was most heinous amongst the offenders and hence there was a national outcry for him to be treated as an adult for some reason or the other and playing on this sentiment Government had to react in some manner or the other and hence it was during Mr. Narendra Modi led – government that on

December 22, 2015 that the Rajya Sabha passed the new Juvenile Justice Bill which allowed the State to try a person between the age of 16 – 18 as an adult if the Court of Law is convinced that the offence committed is heinous in nature. This might have solved the immediate problem of silencing the national outcry and earn some goodwill points for the Government but that is it. By this amendment the State also interfered with one good piece of penal law legislature which concentrated on rehabilitation of offenders.

Similarly to "Whipping Act" of the colonial era, every other penal law made during that period was to control the Indian mass by those belonging to the British Government represented through East India Company in a manner that was most convenient to them. It is important to understand that this was a period when these laws were being made for people who anyway didn't happen to have many rights and a large proportion wasn't aware of it if there were to be any and hence the laws were being made by the masters for their servants to keep them in order, and here order means in the way they fancied and hence the punishments which were an easy way to ensure that the people followed the orders of the British Officials conveniently. First the British, and later on the Aristocrats of India took the convenient method of instilling fear of law among citizens to make sure the order is maintained conveniently. This is because we are obedient to one English scholar, Sir John William Salmond (1862-1924) who many find one of the greatest scholars in the legal field and is said to belong to the Analytical School of Jurisprudence, yet he had different opinions. In his words, an imperative law is —"a percept or rule of action imposed upon man by some authority which enforces obedience to it. In other words, imperative law is the command or a rule in the form of a command which is enforced by some superior power."[26] He also argues that the laws cannot be universal. If that is to be the cases then all of United Nations Conventions are not fit laws? That, Universal Human Rights, which is an extra-ordinary piece of document which tries to ensure basic human rights to all people across the universe. This territorial approach of his allowed his students to think in the similar fashion, that it is a territorial requirement to have punitive measures to maintain law and order like it was maintained during the colonial era. This is also called the Deterrence Theory approach. Deterrence Theory is the theory that criminal penalties do not

---

[26] SAROJ BISTA'S BLOG, *Salmond in Analytical School*, Published on February 22, 2017 Accessed from http://bistasarojlaw.blogspot.com/2017/02/salmond-in-analytical-school.html on 27.07.2020

just punish violators, but also discourage other people from committing similar offenses. Many people point to the need to deter criminal actions after a high – profile incident in which an offender is seen to have received a light sentence. Some argue that a tougher sentence would have prevented the tragedy and can prevent similar tragedy from taking place in the future.[27] This is the theory followed by lawmakers today in this country whenever there is a national outcry on any particular issue pertaining to offence committed by an individual happens.

Indian lawmakers though have tried to keep the law as deterrent as they can by making sure that there are provisions like Capital Punishment to offenders. To show how backward it puts us, statistically saying, according to Amnesty there are 106

---

[27] Ben Johnson, *Do Criminal Laws Deter Crime? Deterrence Theory in Criminal Justice Police: A Primer*, Minnesota House Research Department (January 2019), Accessed from https://www.house.leg.state.mn.us/hrd/pubs/deterrence.pdf on 15.07.2020

countries where use of death penalty is abolished by law, 7 countries which permit the death penalty only for serious crimes in exceptional circumstances, such as those committeed during times of war, and, 29 countries have death penalty laws but haven't executed anyone for at least 10 years, and a policy or a more formal commitment not to execute and lastly there are 56 countries which retain death penalty laws and either carry out executions or the authorities have not made an official declaration not to execute.[28] That tells that a Indian lawmakers still haven't removed it because they feel that there is a need for capital punishment to exist in this society. It is the good faith of Judiciary which has not exponentially used this provision and the last person to be hanged to death before the more recent 4 culprits of

---

[28] BBC Reality Check Team, *Death Penalty: How Many Countries Still Have It?*, 14th October 2018, Accessed from https://www.bbc.com/news/world-45835584 on 15.07.2020

the Delhi Rape Case in 2020 was of Dhananjoy Chatterjee in 2004, 14 years after being accused for rape and murder of a 14 – year old schoolgirl on March 4, 1990.[29] The Capital Punishment is punishment of highest degree and the court has reserved it for rarest of rare circumstances strictly.

Most investigations of punishment appear to accept that it assumes a significant function in molding the behavior of individuals, regardless of whether they are kids, understudies, working adults, or conventional residents of the society. A few people contend that there is no avocation for the utilization of punishment in any setting, in any event, childrearing. A bill discussed in the 2007 California state governing body that would make spanking illegal gives off an impression of being a move toward

[29] Indo-Asian News Service, *16 Convicts hanged to death in India since 1991*, India Today (January 8, 2020), Accessed from https://www.indiatoday.in/india/story/16-convicts-hanged-to-death-india-since-1991-1634925-2020-01-08 on 22.05.2020

this path. Others accept that there are times when punishment is the best and ideal approach to change behavior and without it homes, schools, associations, and social orders would crumble.[30]

There are various punishment theories that have come in at various different times in history as historically there have always been two sides, one that enforces the law and the other on which it is enforced upon and hence the punishment theories prevailed and continues to prosper to date. Although it is believed by a vast number of people that punishment can be effective and can be said to be successful now and again, you can most likely think about a couple of instances of when a punishment doesn't reliably lessen undesirable conduct. Prison is one prime model. Subsequent to being

[30] David J. Cherrington, *Crime and Punishment: Does Punishment Work?*, The Hayes Report on Loss Prevention Volume 22, Issue 2, Hayes International , Fruitland Park, Florida, 1, 27.

released off prison for a wrongdoing, individuals frequently keep perpetrating offences whenever they are released from jail.[31]

Criminal punishment is a primitive approach but deterrence theory is not the way forward either and the same is in no way any form of reformative policy. It has been argued by few scholars as the way forward though, and the classic Plato gave a "classical" theory of deterrence as, "No one punishes the evil-doer under the notion, or for the reason, that he has done wrong, - only the unreasonable fury of a beast acts in that manner. But he who desires to inflict rational punishment does not retaliate for a past wrong which cannot be undone; he has regard to the future, and is desirous that the man who is punished, and he who sees him punished, may be deterred from doing

[31] Fazel S, Wolf A., *A systematic review of criminal recidivism rates worldwide: Current difficulties and recommendations for best practice.* PLoS ONE 2015;10(6):e0130390. doi:10.1371/journal.pone.0130390

wrong again. He punishes for the sake of prevention."[32] I hope that this is the fancy term which is used to define a very basic concept that when the State uses a person to set an example of him by punishing him so hard that others do not dare to commit the same offence that he did. Now, many would question what is wrong with that intention? To them I would like to ask themselves a question, that how this is different from what was done to the Indians by the British officials, or before that by the Mughal empire officials or whoever had control over the territory? They all fancied this method of setting examples through harsh punishments. If this is the method to be adopted, then why fight for freedom? If this is acceptable practice then what was wrong with the British – rule? Didn't the people of India got together to fight against the atrocities

[32] Plato, *Protagoras* 43, Ed. Benjamin Jowett, Serenity Publishers, 2009

led by the British officials on local residents initially? Wasn't injustice and differential behaviour the primary reason the people demanded "SWARAJ"? Theoretically the people got it too. Today, India is a free country and its people are independent of any foreign rule and theoretically it is also a democratic state which has a Constitution. I guess that is why there hasn't been much progress in India in penal laws since independence because today there is no foreigner against whom we people can get together but it is our elected government that continues to use these primitive measures against us itself and since they are one amongst us and so many of them are there that call for positive reforms is something that gets mixed up, nobody wants to talk about it, everyone is happy as long as the culprit is suffering.

In a letter written to Thomas Mercer, former British Parliamentarian Edmund Burke said, "The only thing necessary for the triumph of evil is for good men to do nothing"[33] and that is what happened with Indian Penal laws, the good men who were responsible for drafting the Constitution decided the brutal penal law enforced by the British Government to continue to prevail on the land and hence the evil triumphs to day. I call the penal laws evil because even after completion of the punishment, the person is never actually free. I say this because once sentenced to prison, after completion of the sentencing period and upon being now released a person should be considered reformed if the penal laws are reformative in nature as the Government wants us to believe? But how would he reform when he will face obstacles everywhere due to his

---

[33] Edmund Burke, *Thoughts on the Cause of the Present Discontents*, 82-83 (1770) in: *Select Works of Edmund Burke*, Vol. 1, p.146 (Liberty Fund ed. 1999)

sentencing. A convict in India can not do many things, and will face trouble in almost anything he decides to do. He is not eligible to apply for Government Job vacancies nor can he contest elections, and will face trouble whenever applying for Passport, Visa, any other government document. When a person will face so many obstacles in re-entering the society, his reformation is impossible. Once an accused is convicted of an offence he serves a punishment period for the same offence. Now, upon completion of the punishment for the offence he should be a completely free person, free from the offence at least. His activities may be monitored for security purposes etc., but the person should not suffer any more than his prison period for an offence and only then there is even scope for the reform through deterrence theory to give any positive results. 18th Century philosopher Jeremy Bentham said,

"The first objective is to prevent all sorts of offences as far as this is worthwhile; therefore, the value of the punishment must always be sufficient to outweigh the value of the profit of the offence."[34] To elaborate, Beccaria wrote laws exist to permit a unified society, liberated from the danger of war and mayhem. He accepted that every individual from this general public will "consistently try to detract from the mass, his own share, however to infringe on that of others."[35] Laws were essential, consequently, and an infringement of laws should bring about punishement whose design "is no other, than to keep others from carrying out the like offense."[36] He contended that punishment must be proportionate to

---

[34] Jeremy Bentham, *An Introduction to the Principles of Morals and Legislation (introduction to the Principles)*, Oxford: Clarendon Press, 1907, pg. 179

[35] Cesare Bonesana di Beccaria, "*An Essay on Crimes and Punishment*, By the Marquis Beccarioa of Milan. With a Commentary by M. de Voltaire. A New Edition Corrected," (Albany: W.C. Little & Co., 1872).

[36] Cesare Bonesana di Beccaria, "An *Essay on Crimes and Punishment*, By the Marquis Beccarioa of Milan. With a Commentary by M. de Voltaire. A New Edition Corrected," (Albany: W.C. Little & Co., 1872). Pg. 16

the wrongdoing perpetrated on the grounds that, if two violations have an equivalent punishment, "there isn't anything to prevent men from carrying out the greater" when that wrongdoing conveys a more prominent preferred position.[37] Beccaria additionally underlined that punishment ought to happen as following the commission of a wrongdoing as could reasonably be expected and included that crimes "are more effectually prevented by the certainty, than the severity of punishment."[38]

There is a proverb to say that Punishment governs all mankind; punishment alone preserves them; punishment awakes while their guards are asleep; the wise considers the punishment as the perfection of

---

[37] Cesare Bonesana di Beccaria, *"An Essay on Crimes and Punishment*, By the Marquis Beccarioa of Milan. With a Commentary by M. de Voltaire. A New Edition Corrected," (Albany: W.C. Little & Co., 1872). Pg. 47

[38] Cesare Bonesana di Beccaria, *"An Essay on Crimes and Punishment*, By the Marquis Beccarioa of Milan. With a Commentary by M. de Voltaire. A New Edition Corrected," (Albany: W.C. Little & Co., 1872). Pg. 73,94

justice.[39] The earliest written criminal codes, the Sumerican Code and the Code of Hammurabi specified the concept of "equality of revenge" which when translated means the severity of the punishment must be equal to the severity of the offense. The process of punishing people for their offences in criminal cases is also to bring the sufferers some satisfaction as well. But as famously said, an eye for an eye shall make the whole world blind. The method of inflicting pain so that the convict apparently "learns his lesson" is too primitive an approach but it is what it is when we look at the current situation around us. The deterrence theory has been heavily criticized across the world by various scholars in their numerous works. Likewise there are several theories to support the use of punishment to maintain order in the society which can broadly be classified as (i)

---

[39] Translated by Haughton, G. C. 1835)Ch 7, para 18 p. 189.

utilitarian, or, (ii) retributive. Under the utilitarian philosophy,laws that indicate punishment for criminal conduct ought to prevent future criminal conduct. Deterrence works on a particular and an overall level. General implies that the punishment ought to keep others from perpetrating criminal acts. This fills in as an illustration to the remainder of the general public, and it notifies others that criminal conduct must be punished.

Justice A. K. Sikri while passing an order stated the state of sentencing policies in our country by emphasizing upon that in various countries, sentencing guidelines are provided, statutorily or otherwise, which may guide Judges for awarding specific sentence, in India we do not have any such sentencing policy till date. The prevalence of such guidelines may not only aim at achieving consistencies in awarding sentences in different cases, such guidelines normally prescribe the sentencing policy as well, namely, whether the purpose of awarding punishment in a particular case is more of a deterrence or retribution or rehabilitation, etc. In the absence of such guidelines in India, the courts go by their own perception about the philosophy behind the prescription of certain specified penal consequences for particular nature of crime. For some deterrence and/or vengeance becomes more important whereas another Judge may be more influenced by rehabilitation or restoration as the goal of sentencing. Sometimes, it would be a combination of both which would weigh in the mind of the court in awarding a particular sentence. However, that may be a question of quantum.[40]

The criminal laws in the country not only create a burden on the judicial

---

[40] State of Himachal Pradesh vs. Nirmala Devi, SC Crl. App. No. 667 of 2017, April 10, 2017.

system of the country but also overcrowd the prisons in the country. The Apex Court had observed in February, 2020 that the current 1,341 prisons in the country was holding 4.68 lakh prisoners whereas the permissible limit for the combined prisons stands at 3.83 lakh. A large proportion of this number is of undertrials. According to NCRB figures only a 1/3 number of prisoners are convicted offenders and the rest are undertrials and a staggering 84% of total inmates in Bihar are that of undertrials. This is an alarming number and this happens because a large section is not aware of their legal rights and it here where legal aid centers play an important role in providing such people justice. The Apex Court has already said that a free legal assistance at State cost is a fundamental right of a person accused of an offence[41] and that if the

Government fails to conduct a trial within reasonable time, it violates the guarantee of the life and personal liberty enshrined in Article 21.[42] Justice Bhagwati in Hussainara Khatoon said that unlike the American Constitution speedy trial is not specially enumerated as a fundamental right, but it is implicit in the broad sweep and content of Article 21 as interpreted in Maneka Gandhi's[43] case and that no procedure which does not ensure a reasonably quick trial can be regarded as reasonable, fair and just. Through the judgment Justice Bhagwati ordered to conduct a survey which found 21,000 undertrial prisoners languishing in prisons who have had spent the maximum period of imprisonment for their alleged offence and were ordered to be freed on their personal bond, and about

---

[41] Sukdas Vs. Arunachal Pradesh, AIR 1986 SC 991
[42] Hussainara Khatoon Vs. State of Bihar, AIR 1979 SC 1360
[43] Maneka Gandhi Vs. Union of India, 1978 SCR (2) 621

18,000 of the 21,000 inmates were from various prisons of State of Bihar. Overcrowding and understaffing in prisons in India often leads to mismanagement in prisons and often becomes difficult for prison executives to maintain the minimum basic standards of prison environment and often leads to people falling sick in prisons. A team of the Jharkhand People's Union for Civil Liberties (PUCL) visited Sakchi jail, East Singhbhum, Jharkhand and created a report citing how pathetic and highly condemnable conditions are at the prison and had sent it to National Human Rights Commission[44]. Considering the ailing conditions of prisoners the Gujrat High Court directed the jail authorities to take proper care of ailing convicts[45] in Rasikbhai Rana Case. A major step was taken in R.D. Upadhyay's[46] case

---

[44] http://www.pucl.org/Topics/Prisons?2007/sakchi.html
[45] Rasikbhai Ramsing Rana Vs. State of Gujrat, (DB) 1997 Cr LR (Guj) 442
[46] R.D. Upadhyay Vs. State of A.P. and Ors., AIR 2006 SC 1946

when the apex court set guidelines for pregnant inmates. The Hon'ble Supreme Court directed that before sending a pregnant woman to a jail, the concerned authorities must ensure that the jail where she is to stay at has the basic minimum facilities for delivery of a child as well as for providing pre-natal and post-natal care for both, the mother and the child. The court was of the following opinion;

"In light of various reports referred to above, affidavits of various State Governments, Union Territories, Union of India and submissions made, we issue the following guidelines:

1.   A child shall not be treated as an undertrial/convict while in jail with his/her mother. Such a child is entitled to food, shelter, medical care, clothing, education and recreational facilities as a matter of right."

And an exhaustive list of guidelines were given which ensured the protection of a pregnant woman and that of her kid in the light of growing number of custodial violence on women inmates[47]

Oscar Wilde once said that it is not the prisoners who need reformation but it is the prisons[48] and time and again the Indian Judicial system through its various judgments has tried to intervene in how prisons are run in this country. It so happened that Justice Krishna Iyer who was among the judges in Sunil Batra[49] case wherein the scope of the writ of habeas corpus was expanded by recognizing the right of an inmate to invoke the writ against prison atrocities inflicted upon him or on a co-prisoner. The court in the case had

[47] Sheela Barse Vs. State of Maharashtra, AIR 1983 SC 378

[48] Martyn Housden, 'Oscar Wilde's imprisonment and an early idea of "Banal Evil" 'or 'Two "wasps" in the system How Reverend W.D. Morrison and Oscar Wilde challenged penal policy in late Victorian England', 25 October, 2006 in forum historiae iuris, https://forhistiur.de/2006-10-housden/

[49] Sunil Batra- I and II Vs. Delhi Administration 1978 Cri. LJ 1741 at 1795 SC, 1980 Cri. LJ 1099 at 1114

given directions to the prison executives to treat the prisoners with human dignity. Certain guidelines were mentioned alongwith this judgment like periodical visits by lawyers, District Magistrates, etc., and insisted that the judicial officers referred to by them shall carry out their duties and responsibilities and serve as an effective Grievance Mechanism. The court has time and again emphasized upon the fact that the convicts are not denuded of all the fundamental rights which they otherwise possess. A compulsion, following upon conviction, to live in a prison house entails by its own force the deprivation of fundamental freedoms like right to move freely throughout the territory of India or the rights to practice a profession but his other constitutionally guaranteed precious rights under Article 21 are still applicable to the convicts that he shall not be deprived of his life and personal liberty except according to the procedure established by law[50] and that imprisonment does not spell farewell to fundamental rights[51] altogether.

The apex court has never shied itself away from acting like an ombudsman and policing the police as it expressed its anguish over police torture in Raghubir Singh's[52] case by upholding the sentence awarded to a police officer responsible for the death of an alleged suspect due to torture in police custody. But the process of interrogation should've been questioned rather than the validity of judgment. One needs to know why were such measures being taken by police officers during the investigation process and wasn't there other possible methods, a way in which one does not need to be physically assaulted.

---

[50] D.B.M. Patnaik Vs. State of Andhra Pradesh, 1974 SC AIR 2092
[51] Charles Sobraj Vs. Supdt Central Jail Tihar, AIR 1978 SC 1514
[52] Raghubir Singh Vs. State of Bihar, (1986) 4 SCC 481

With the above mentioned anecdotes from the Judicial history of dealing with prisons tells that both the law of crimes and the law of prison, i.e., Indian Penal Code and the Indian Prison's Act are both acts enacted in a pre-independent country and hence the current laws should be in light of the Indian Constitution, one which safeguards the principles of the Constitution and a law of crimes and prisons which reflect the principles of our Constitution in it and not one which smells of colonial era. It's about time that the laws are made considering safeguarding the individuals interest above the interests of the State. The laws should be such that protects the individual's rights and not one that becomes a tool or a weapon for the State to use against individuals for whatsoever reason until and unless it is not for the benefit of the society. Laws like sedition and contempt are violating of the basic right of freedom of free speech, and if in a democratic country where criticism can amount to imprisonment, that country should not be termed as a democratic republic because it is very much an authoritative democratic in current scenario wherein people can change the people at the government (so far) but are held in prison when try to raise a voice against the government and the only form of showing dissent left for the mass is through Voting powers but when both sides are of the same coin somebody needs to tell the umpire to change the coin for the toss, that voice should not be suppressed and met with punitive measures because if that voice is silenced then that would be a death of the Constitution.

This country is for the people, by the people and of the people of this country and the penal laws should be to protect the people of this country exercising their rights and duties so that analogies like deprivation of life is constitutionally permissible for being recognized as a permissible punishment by the drafters of the constitution[53] can be spared for the future generations to come.

---

[53] Jagmohan Singh Vs. State of U.P., AIR 1973 SC 947

Chapter 3: The Land of Gandhi

Mahatma Gandhi strongly opposed punitive measures taken on wrongdoers as he was a sufferer himself of that system. He always thought of criminals as patients. In a public meeting he said, "In independence India of the non-violent type, there will be crime but no criminals. They will not be punished. Crime is a disease like any other malady and is a product of the prevalent social system. Therefore, all crime including murder will be treated as a disease. Whether such as India will ever come into being is another question".[54] He expressed his desire for a better society by continue saying, "What should our jails be like in free India? All criminals should be treated as patients and the jails should be hospitals admitting the

[54] The Selected Works of Mahatma Gandhi, Vol. V – The Voice of Truth, Part II – Section IX : Political Ideas, The Police, Crimes and Jails., p. 69

class of patients for treatment and cure. No one commits crime for the fun of it. It is a sign of a diseased mind. The causes of a particular disease should be investigated and removed. They need not have palatial buildings when their jails become hospitals. No country can afford that, much less can a poor country like India. But the outlook of the jail staff should be that of physicians and nurses in a hospital. The prisoners should feel that the officials are their friends. They are there to help them regain their mental health and not to harass them in any way. The popular governments have to issue necessary orders, but meanwhile the jail staff can do not a little to humanize their administration".

Not just Gandhi, but many scholars have argued over the time that measures taken for rehabilitation and social improvement of prisoners have shown positive results and hence is claimed to be the right way forward. This is the introduction to how the punitive system can be replaced with a prison system which actually works and helps in reducing crime in the society.

Rehabilitation is defined as "a set of interventions designed to optimize functioning and reduce disability in individuals with health conditions in interaction with their environment". Helping wrongdoers in becoming pro-social residents has been a major task of criminologists, psychologists, psychiatrists and other related experts for longer than a century. Endeavors to diminish re-culpable and increment pro-social conduct are found essentially in the criminal justice framework and the accomplishment in accomplishing these two objectives has been tricky. The expression rehabilitation literally might refer to restoration of something to its proper condition, although, in the criminal justice context, one might say that this would normally involve intervention to help offenders to adopt law-abiding lives and to turn away from unlawful activities. Importantly, the term rehabilitation has now replaced treatment, which was in common use in the 1970s and 1980s and which served to forge a close association with the medical treatment paradigm. In that period (roughly from the mid-1970s to the mid 1990s) numerous analysts and experts believed that little should be possible to rehabilitate wrongdoers. Nonetheless, the 1990s saw a surge of new research and investigation that yielded a significantly more hopeful perspective on the viability of certain methods to change the conduct of guilty parties towards more pro-social practices.[55] Some of these methods

---

[55] Bonta, J. & Andrews, D. A. (2007). Risk-need-responsivity model for offender assessment and rehabilitation. (User Report No. 2007-06). Ottawa: Public Safety Canada.

show hope in reviving the maligned image of prison system. These methods focus on social improvement steps to be taken during the course of rehabilitation of the prisoner.

Rehabilitation Psychology is a specialty area under psychology which concerns itself with the study and application of psychological knowledge and skills on behalf of individuals with disabilities and chronic health conditions with the objective to maximize health and welfare, independence and choice, functional abilities, and social role participation, across the lifespan[56]. Experts in the field known as Rehabilitation Psychologists are uniquely trained and specialized to engage in a broad range of activities including clinical practice, consultation, program development, service provision, research, teaching

[56] Allen Heinemann, *Rehabilitation Psychology*, Encyclopedia Britannica, December 28, 2018. Available on https://www.britannica.com/science/rehabilitation-psychology, Accessed on November 17, 2020.

and education, training, administration and development of public policy and advocacy related to persons with disability and chronic health conditions. Rehabilitation psychologists, often within teams, assess and treat cognitive, emotional, and functional difficulties, and help people to overcome barriers to participation in life activities[57]. Rehabilitation psychologists are present in a wide range of institutions already serving individuals living with disabling conditions, including hospitals, universities, medical schools, schools, not for profit organizations, and central and state agencies.[58]

With over 50 years of organized professional involvement, rehabilitation psychology is one of the oldest psychological specialties active

[57] American Psychological Association, *Rehabilitation Psychology*, accessed from https://www.apa.org/ed/graduate/specialize/rehabilitation on 27.04.2020
[58] Awasthi, Purnima & Yadava, Vibha & Pandey, Ravi. (2016). *Disability, Rehabilitation and Rehabilitation Psychology: An Overview*, Indian Journal of Community Psychology. Vol. 12, p. 196-210

in interdisciplinary medical settings, health and public policy, and the study of and service to persons with disabling health conditions.

Open any book on crime and punishment today and one of the initial chapters shall include a discussion of the decline pf the rehabilitative idea and the shift towards a more punitive criminal justice system. Gone are the days of 'Bail, not Jail!' philosophy. One reason for this is that the rehabilitative idea was discredited due to a lack of evidence that prison treatment programs could result in reducing recidivism. But, the primary purpose of imprisonment yet remains to protect the society against crime and to reduce recidivism. International standards make it clear that these can only be achieved if the time in prison is used to ensure the reintegration of prisoners into society upon release, so that they can lead law –abiding and self-supporting lives.[59]

Sometimes, Criminal Rehabilitation can happen through Medical Intervention too. The medical model of intervention as a form of rehabilitation emerged at the turn of the century in response to the perceived ineffectiveness of early means of reform that used labor and physical punishments to change people's behavior. New "scientific" disciplines like psychiatry, psychology, and criminology proposed that the causes of crime and deviance could be linked to biological, physiological, or psychological defects of the individual. Criminals need to be viewed as products of socioeconomic or psychological forces beyond their control and in a way undergoing a "sickness" and hence the objective shall shift to "cure" the offender.[60] To find the cure, the

---

[59] United Nations Standard Minimum Rules for the Treatment of Prisoners (the Nelson Mandela Rules), Rule 4

patients need to be segregated in groups, groups of particular kind. For example people suffering from drug abuse, or sex offenders, etc are broad categories under which people can be treated for their type of sickness. Like the rehabilitation and management of sex offenders shall be different to a drug addict in many ways. The rehabilitation and management of sex offenders presents considerable challenges within a custodial environment. Not only are sex offenders heterogeneous, but numerous theoretical models have been proposed to explain sexual offending with comprehensive models integrating developmental, psychosocial, environmental and physiological, environmental and physiological factors. There is, however a theoretical consensus that the behaviour is learned and, as such, is amenable to change.

---

[60] Becci I., Roy O. (eds) Religious Diversity in European Prisons. Springer, Cham. https://doi.org/10.1007/978-3-319-16778-7_1

A number of other issues routinely arise in the rehabilitation of sex offenders, for which there is little empirical evidence to guide practice. These include whether programs should mix or separate child molesters and rapists,[61] how those who categorically deny offending should be managed,[62] the use of preparatory programs should address non-criminogenic human needs.[63] Many treatment programmes for sexual offenders place all of these clients in the same group, where they receive the same treatment components over the same period of time.[64] Since sexual offenders display heterogeneity across every aspect of their history, personal characteristics,

---

[61] Polaschek, Devon & King, Lucy. (2002), *Rehabilitating Rapists: Reconsidering the Issues*, Australian Psychologist – AUST PSYCHOL, Vol. 37, p. 215-221

[62] Marshall, W.L. & Marshall, Liam & Fernandez, Yolanda & Thornton, David & Mann, Ruth. (2001). *Treatment of Sexual Offenders Who Are in Categorical Denail: A Pilot Project*, Vol. 13, doi 10.1177/107906320101300305

[63] Ward, Tony & Stewart, Claire. (2003). *The treatment of Sex Offenders: Risk Management and Good Lives*. Professional Psychology: Research and Practice. Vol 34, p. 353-360. doi 10.1037/0735-7028.34.4.353

[64] Laws, D. R. & O'Donohue, W. T. (Eds.). (2008). *Sexual Deviance: Theory, Assessment, and Treatment* (2nd ed.). The Guilford Press

and sexual interests that have been evaluated,[65] it makes no sense to treat them all the same. In order to better allocate sexual offenders to treatment programmes that best meet their needs, some pre-treatment assessments are necessary.

While many programmes prior to treatment, engage in extensive assessments[66] or in an elaborate case-formulation for each offender[67] it is not clear that such comprehensive pre-treatment evaluations are either necessary or sufficient. There are numerous examples of unproven methods used in the rehabilitation of those with sexual convictions. Such practices tend to be based on "intuitive beliefs" such as it "feels right", but there is little evidence they

[65] Fernandez, Yolanda & Shingler, Jo & Marshall, W.. (2008). *Putting "Behavior" Back into the Cognitive-Behavioral Treatment of Sexual Offenders.* Sexual Offender Treatment: Controversial Issues. P. 211-224, doi 10.1002/9780470713457. ch 15.
[66] Barbaree, H. E., & Seto, M. C. (1997). *Pedophilia: Assessment and Treatment.* The Guilford Press, p. 175-193
[67] Drake, C. R., & Ward, T. (2003). *Treatment models for sex offenders: A move toward formulation-based approach*, Thousand Oaks, CA. Sage Publications. P. 226-243

reduce recidivism. Some of the traditional approaches to working with people with sexual convictions have an unproven evidence base. These include programmes that focus on encouraging victim empathy and tackling denial, rather than on skills to lead a good and better life. While getting a person to admit to their offending feels right, for example, it's not related to reducing recidivism.

In general, in correctional intervention with offenders, specific principles have been found to be essential in interventions designed to reduce recidivism, and specifically, the principles of risk, need, and responsivity. While originally intended to be applied predominantly to criminal justice sanctions, in practice this model has additionally been applied to treatment, and perhaps more so to treatment than to sanctions.

According to risk principle, the intensity of correctional interventions must be matched to the level of risk posed by the offender. Treatment as well as supervision, should be longer in duration, applied more frequently, and include more contact hours as assessed risk to reoffend increases.[68] Thus, the most intensive levels of service should be reserved for higher risk offenders, while lower levels of intervention should be applied to lower risk offenders. In fact, low risk offenders likely do not require specialized treatment at all, and will benefit from routine supervision.[69] Adherence to the risk principle, in addition of being the best use of limited resources, demonstrates that treatment is most effective when its level of intensity is matched to risk.[70]

[68] Lowencamp, C. T., Latessa, E. & Holsinger, A. (2006). *The risk principle in action: What have we learned from 13,676 offenders and 97 correctional programs?*. Sage Journals. Vol. 52, Isue 1, p 77-93

[69] Hanson, R. Karl & Yates, Pamela. (2013). *Psychological Treatment of Sex Offenders*. Current psychiatry reports. Vol. 15. p 348. doi 10.1007/s11920-012-0348-x.

[70] Nicholaichuk, T., Gordon, A., Gu, D. et al. *Outcome of an Institutional Sexual*

That is when higher risk offenders receive higher intensity treatment, and moderate risk offenders receive intervention at more moderate levels of intensity, the impact on reduced recidivism is greatest. Furthermore, research indicates that, when risk and treatment intensity are not appropriately matched, recidivism can increase as a function of treatment, as in the case of lower risk offenders who receive treatment at an intensity that is greater than required to address their needs.[71]

Among sexual offenders, specific static and dynamic risk factors have been associated with increased risk of recidivism. Static risk factors – those that cannot be changed through intervention – include younger age, previous sexual offences, the

---

Offender Treatment Program: A Comparison Between Treated and Matched Untreated Offenders. Sex Abuse, Vol. 12, p. 139-153. doi 10.1023/A:1009542208305

[71] Lowenkemp, C. T., & Latessa, E. J. (2002). Evaluation of Ohio's Community based correctional facilities and halfway house programs [Technical report]. Cincinnati, OH: University of Cincinnati

commission of non-contact sexual offences and non-sexual violent offences, and offending against male victims, unrelated victims, and strangers.[72] Dynamic risk factors are discussed below.

When considering treatment intensity, little research has been conducted regarding the most appropriate length of intervention, and practice varies substantially across jurisdictions.[73] Some programs recommend between 80 and 120 contact hours, while others recommend between 160-195 contact hours for moderate risk sexual offenders and approximately 300 hours of treatment contact for high risk offenders. In a comprehensive evaluation, Bourgon and Armstrong examined treatment intensity as a

[72] Hanson, R. K., & Thornton, D. (1999). *Static-99: Improving actual risk assessments for sex offenders* (User Report 99-02). Ottawa: Department of the Solicitor General of Canada

[73] McGrath J, Brown A, St Clair D. *Prevention and schizophrenia—the role of dietary factors*. Schizophr Bull. 2011 Mar: 37(2):272-83 doi: 10.1093/schbul/sbq121. Epub 2010 Oct 25. PMID: 20974747; PMCID: PMC3044637

function of both risk and criminogenic needs.[74] They found that 100 contact hours was sufficient to reduce recidivism for general offenders presenting with moderate risk and few criminogenic needs, 200 hours was more effective when offenders were either high risk or had multiple criminogenic needs, and that 300 contact hours or more was required to reduce recidivism among offenders who were both higher risk and who had multiple criminogenic needs. Based on research pertaining to general offenders, as well as results from accredited sexual offender programs, Hanson and Yates recommend that no special treatment for low risk sexual offenders,[75] which should roughly be the bottom 10% to 20% of the risk distribution, 100 to

[74] Bourgon, Guy & Armstrong, Barbara. (2005). *Transferring the Principle of Effective Treatment into a "Real World" Prison Setting.* Criminal Justice and Behavior. Vol. 32, p. 3-25, doi: 10.1177/0093854804270618

[75] Hanson RK, Yates PM, *Psychological Treatment of Sex Offenders.* Curr Psycjiatry Rep. 2013 Mar 15(3):348. doi: 10.1007/s11920-012-0348-x. PMID: 23389775

200 contact hours for moderate risk sexual offenders, and a minimum of 300 hours for sexual offenders presenting with high risk and high needs, which should be the top 10% to 20% of the risk distribution.

The second principle of effective correctional intervention, the need principle, states that treatment and interventions such as supervision should explicitly target the criminogenic needs of offenders – that is, the specific risk factors that can be changed through intervention (i.e., dynamic risk factors) and that are empirically associated with recidivism risk. Targeting these risk factors for change leads to reduced re-offending. Research shows that, among sexual wrongdoers, criminogenic needs incorporate such dangerous factors as sexual aberrance and anti-social way of life, the two most grounded indicators of recidivism among sexual offenders.[76] It is critical to note here that examination has consistently found that sexual guilty parties are more probable to reoffend with offenses that are non-sexual in nature than to commit new sexual offenses. Likewise, research demonstrates that the indicators of recidivism are distinctive for various kinds of re-offending. That is, while the most strong indicators of sexual recidivism among sexual wrongdoers incorporate freak sexual interest and withdrawn direction/way of life (standoffish character, introverted attributes, a background marked by rule infringement, and self-guideline issues, for example, impulsivity, way of life flimsiness, and a past filled with non-sexual criminal culpable), sexual aberrance has been discovered to be disconnected to brutal non-sexual offending. Hence, while deciding criminogenic needs that require to be focused during

[76] Hanson, R. Karl & Morton-Bourgon, Kelly. (2004). *Predictors of Sexual Recidivism: An Updated Meta-Analysis*

treatment, it is imperative to take care of the sort of recidivism that is probably going to oc-dog, and to tailor treatment appropriately.

Latest research has furthermore exhibited specific dynamic danger factors that are related with recidivism among sexual offenders. These incorporate degenerate sexual inclinations, an absence of positive social impacts, intimacy shortages, issues with sexual self-guideline, issues with general self-regulation, perspectives of rape, and issues with participation in supervision.[77] In treatment, it is recommended that these be assessed *a priori*, and included as appropriate in individualized treatment plans, along with assessment of static risk in order to determine treatment intensity by these factors in combination.[78]

---

[77] Hanson, R. Karl & Helmus, Leslie Maaike & Harris, Andrew. (2015) *Assessing the Risk and Needs of Supervised Sexual Offenders: A Prospective Study Using STABLE-2007, Static-99R, and Static-2002R*. Criminal Justice and Behavior. 42. doi: 10.1177/0093854815602094

[78] Yates, P. M., Prescott, D. S., & Ward, T. (2010) *Applying the Good Lives and*

Adding to guaranteeing that factors obsessionally-identified with danger of recidivism are attended to, the need principle likewise indicates that treatment ought not zero in on non-criminogenic needs - factors not discovered to be related with recidivism - as this expends resources on attending to factors that are unlikable to bring about reduced re-offending.[79] Non-criminogenic factors incorporate such territories as confidence, individual pain, casualty sympathy, and forswearing, none of which has been discovered to be dependably connected to recidivism in research. While it is normal practice in treatment to address such factors, these are not observations upheld and are probably not going to be the best utilization of restricted resources that expect to lessen re-offending.[80]

Self Regulation Models to sex offender treatment: a practical guide for clinicians. Brandon, VT: Safer Society Press

[79] Andrews, D. A., & Bonta, J. (2010). *Rehabilitating criminal justice policy and practice.* Psychology, Public Policy, and Law, 16(1). p 39-55. doi: 10.1037/a0018362

The third principle of effective correctional intervention, the *responsivity principle*, concerns the interaction between the individual and treatment. Specifically, this principle indicates that treatment, in addition to being cognitive-behavioral in orientation, ought to be conveyed in a way that is receptive to different qualities of the individual, for example, language, culture, character style, knowledge, nervousness levels, learning styles, and intellectual capacities, to expand their commitment and investment in treatment to guarantee maximal viability. These factors can influence individuals' commitment with treatment, their inspiration, their capacity to comprehend and apply knowledge introduced in treatment to their very own conditions, and their way of handling knowledge

---

[80] Hanson, R.Karl & Bussiere, Monique. (1998). *Predicting relapse: A meta-analysis of sexual offender recidivism studies.* Journal of Consulting and Clinical Psychology, 66, p 348-362. doi: 10.1037/0022-006X.66.2.348

introduced in treatment. Subsequently, treatment execution ought to be shifted and adjusted to singular styles and capacities to amplify viability, which includes huge expertise with respect to clinicians.[81] Research support is solid for the utilization of the RNR model and its standards, and demonstrates that treatment with regards to these standards is better than treatment that doesn't adhere to these standards and to criminal punishments alone. In particular, meta-analytic research plainly demonstrates that adherence to this model is successful for intervention with offenders by and large, youth offenders, violent offenders, and female offenders.[82] Critically, adherence to these standards likewise

[81] Andrews, D. A., & Bonta, J. (2010). *Rehabilitating criminal justice policy and practice.* Psychology, Public Policy, and Law, 16(1). p 39-55. doi: 10.1037/a0018362

[82] Dowden, Craig & Antonowicz, Daniel & Andrews, DA (2003). *The Effectiveness of Relapse Prevention with Offenders: A Meta-Analysis.* International journal of offender therapy and comparative criminology. 47. 516-28. doi: 10.1177/0306624X03253018.

applies to the treatment of sexual offenders. In particular, meta-analytic research shows that, when treatment holds up to these standards, it is related with decreased sexual re-offending. The main treatment impact has been found among treatment programs that clung to each of the three standards, also, treatment viability increments as an element of adherence to standards (chances proportions of 1.17, .64, .63, and .21, individually for adherence to each of the three standards, just two, just one, and no adherence). The chances proportion is the probability of an occasion happening or not happening, and for this situation it shows that treatment was best when it clung to every one of the three principles, and diminished logically in viability when treatment clung to less standards.

Violent wrongdoers are in some cases treated as a 'homogenized' group, yet there are various sorts of brutal crimes, various kinds of vicious offender and various groups of experts working with people who have submitted to violent acts. There are likewise lawful meanings of viciousness that will be of incredible importance for the future administration of individual wrongdoers. Violent behaviour can be sorted by offense type. It can likewise be arranged by the inspirations for the demonstration, or by the circumstance and connections that encompass it. Violence inside a domestic setting among family members and private accomplices for instance would be a particular class. Now and again this group is barred from surveys about violent behaviour more generally.[83] Violence against other from groups different to the perpetrator may be considered as a

[83] Jolliffe, D. Farrington, D. (2007) *A systematic review of the national and international evidence on the effectiveness of interventions with violent offenders.* London Ministry of Justice, 2, 60.

separate phenomenon,[84] and is often referred to as hate crime. Violent conduct has additionally been ordered as dependent on the essential driver for the violent act, with a differentiation drawn between receptive rather than proactive conduct, and among incautious and planned activities. These two arrangements of qualifications have been considered to have a few likenesses with one another. Anyway it has been discovered that responsive and impulsive aggression correspond all the more intently, than proactive and planned violence.[85]

There is a few, yet restricted, proof of what is compelling in conveying interventions with violent wrongdoers. Interventions need to establish connection to the assessment of the

[84] De Wall, CN. Anderson, CA. (2011) *The General Aggression Model: Theoretical Extensions to Violence*, Psychology of Violence, Vol. 1, No. 3, 245-258

[85] Babcock, J.C. Tharp, A.L.T. Sharp, C. Heppner, W. and Stanford, M. (2014) *Similarities and Differences in impulsive/premeditated and reactive/proactive bimodal classifications of aggression.* Aggression and Violent Behavior, Volume 19, Issue 3, pp. 251-262

risk factors identified with the probability of future violence. A review[86] found that interventions with violent offenders were effective, with a difference in the percentage reconvicted of about eight to eleven per cent for general re-offending measures and seven to eight per cent for violent re-offending measures. The authors portray the outcomes as promising yet in addition recognize that not many appropriate investigations were accessible for consideration. The study additionally found that the focal point of intervention was critical with general schooling and sympathy lessening the handiness, however with psychological abilities, outrage control, utilization of pretend and relapse avoidance and homework demonstrating more successful. Findings proposed that emotional

[86] Jolliffe, D. Farrington, D. (2007) *A systematic review of the national and international evidence on the effectiveness of interventions with violent offenders.* London Ministry of Justice, 2, 60.

self-administration, relational abilities, social critical thinking and unified training approaches show primarily positive outcomes with a sensibly serious level of dependability. Findings are more fragile as for aggressive behavior at home and less steady regarding prison based programmes.[87]

The question is raised not just of what works, but how interventions work, in other words the importance of a treatment theory that understands the mechanisms that underlie the positive effects. In the Jolliffe and Farrington study why was education counterproductive? McGuire suggests that it may be because it takes time away from more effective elements.

Pundits alert against too thin a dependence on cognitive behavioural approaches. McGuire proposes that

---

[87] Bowen, E. Gilchrist, EA, and Beech, AR (2005) *An examination of the impact of community-based rehabilitation on the offending behaviour of male domestic violence offenders and the characteristics associated with recidivism.* Legal and Criminological Psychology, 10, pp. 189-209

only interventions which join a scope of various procedures (multi modular) should be thought of. Drawing on the General Aggression Model others recommend that customary cognitive-behavioural approaches may not be sufficient to assist people deal with entrenched patterns of thinking particularly if anger is impacting upon their ability to think. They suggest that a clearer understanding of the contributions of values and goals to aggressive behaviour would be helpful.[88] The use of implicit theories to consider the need for a holistic approach to interventions emerges from the literature. It is, for example, acknowledged by those who support interventions focused on anger control, that 'The provision of anger control treatment is an adjunctive therapy. Especially with

[88] Gilbert, F. and Daffern, M. (2010) *Integrating contemporary aggression theory with violent offender treatment: How thoroughly do interventions target violent behaviour?* Aggression and Violent Behaviour, 15, pp. 167-180

forensic populations it is best done as part of a multifaceted treatment programme'.[89] This topic of rehabilitation that are multi-faceted is found in a further review proposing that successful intercessions for guilty parties are customized to the individual, and that psychological conduct treatments and multi-foundational treatments (MST)are effective. This theme of interventions that are multi-faceted is found in a further survey recommending that effective interventions for wrongdoers are custom-made to the individual and that cognitive behavioral treatment and multi-systematic treatments (MST) are viable.[90]

The components of treatment that are good for wrongdoers with psychopathic characteristics require

[89] Novaco, RW. (2013) *Reducing Anger-Related Offending What Works*. In Craig, L Dixon, L. and Gannon, T. What Works in Offender Rehabilitation, Wiley Blackwell

[90] Rubin, J Gallo, F and Coutts, A (2008) *Risk Models Effective Interventions and Risk Management*, available at https://www.nao.org.uk/wp-content/uploads/2008/02/0708241_risk_models.pdf, Accessed on 22.11.2020

further study.[91] Of note is the Violence Reduction Program which has some observational help. It is expected for medium to high risk non sexual violent wrongdoers, excluding domestic violence, however incorporating those with psychopathic attributes. Again it utilizes a cognitive behavioral approach, but also stresses the wider environment, and the importance of social influences, including for example the influence of prison staff. It is flexible in delivery with no fixed number of sessions, instead focusing on achieving specific treatment goals 'Results of programme evaluations with long-term follow-up and the inclusion of control groups indicate that programme participation was linked to the reduction of general and violent re-offending.[92]

[91] Egan, V. (2013) *What Works for Personality Disordered Offenders*. In Craig, L. Dixon, L. and Gannon, T. *What Works in Offender Rehabilitation*, Wiley Blackwell
[92] Stephen C.P. Wong, SCP and Gordon, A. (2013) *The Violence Reduction*

The specific issue of locating treatment in prison environments also needs further study but the potential negative impact of unhelpful custodial environments is supported. A study found that the experience of being made to 'feel small' or 'invisible' within the prison context raises the risk that prisoners will engage in violence or aggression.[93] Work looking at therapeutic communities within prisons is included below and also raises concerns about the extent to which the environment within which work is delivered, makes a difference to effectiveness issues which might be of importance include'a perceived lack of safety, poor facilities, security versus therapy disputes, adversarial staff-service user relationships, the pejorative labelling of those in treatment,

Programme: a treatment programme for violence-prone forensic clients, Psychology, Crime & Law, 19:5-6, pp.461-475.
[93] Butler, M., & Maruna, S. (2009). The impact of disrespect on prisoners' aggression: Outcomes of experim68entally inducing violence-supportive cognitions. Psychology, Crime and Law, 15, 235–250

and the reinforcement of non-engagement within the informal institutional culture'.[94]

Another way to conduct interventions for violent offenders inside custodial foundations draws on the ideas of therapeutic communities.[95] There is limited evaluation of the impact of these communities on re-offending.[96] While CBT and TC have developed separately it is suggested that there may be ways in which they fit with and support each other in effect doubling the dosage of interventions. Further work is needed to look at this in more detail.

A recent study looked at the evidence for long-term treatment of personality disordered offenders in hospital using a modified therapeutic

[94] Day, A. Doyle, P. (2010) *Violent offender rehabilitation and the therapeutic community model of treatment: Towards integrated service provision?* Aggression and Violent Behavior, 15,pp.380-386.

[95] Stevens, A. (2014) *Difference and Desistance in Prison Based Therapeutic Communities*, Prison Service Journal, 213, p.3-9.

[96] Jolliffe, D. Farrington, D. (2007) *A systematic review of the national and international evidence on the effectiveness of interventions with violent offenders.* London Ministry of Justice, 2, 60.

community model.[97] This modified community included accredited offending behaviour programmes and found significant positive change between assessment and discharge in violence risk. It is also suggested that TCs fit and overlap with approaches to offender rehabilitation rooted in ideas of desistance from offending and with the good lives model discussed later.[98] There is increasing interest in the importance of understanding the processes by which offenders desist from offending. Desistance is now generally seen as a process that takes place over time rather than as a discrete event.[99] This body of theory and research has not generally concentrated on high risk

[97] Wilson, K., Freestone, M., Taylor, C., Blazey, F., and Hardmand, F. (2014) *Effectiveness of modified therapeutic community treatment within a medium-secure service for personality-disordered offenders*, Journal of Forensic Psychiatry & Psychology, 25, pp.243-261.
[98] Stevens, A. (2014) *Difference and Desistance in Prison Based Therapeutic Communities*, Prison Service Journal, 213, p.3-9.
[99] Healy, D. (2010) The Dynamics of Desistance: charting pathways to change. Willan.

violent offenders but it is suggested that while there is limited empirical research, desistance literature is of significance for the community management of high risk offenders.[100] One study suggests that work with domestically abusive men needs to be substantially more focused on the process of desistance and supports the idea that change from an offending to a non-offending identity should be seen as a process that needs to be supported over time.[101] One part of desistance with connections to the thoughts of TCs is that of personality change.[102] It is possible that time in a TC can give an occasion to change to build up another content or biography.

[100] Weaver, B (2014) Control or change? Developing dialogues between desistance research and public protection practices, Probation Journal, 2014, 61, pp.8-26.

[101] Morran, D. (2013) *Desisting from Domestic Abuse: Influences, Patterns and Processes in the Lives of Formerly Abusive Men*, The Howard Journal Vol 52 No 3. pp. 306-320

[102] Giordano,P.C., Cernkovich, S.A., and Rudolph, J.L. (2002) *Gender, Crime and Desistance: Towards a Theory of Cognitive Transformation*, American Journal of Sociology, 107, pp.990-1064.

Wrongdoers have been found to portray their contact with probation officers as simple reporting, feeling that there was little help for them to quit the criminal lifestyle.

It is important to acknowledge that most violent offenders commit a range of other offences and there is no reason why the findings of the desistance literature should not be of relevance.[103] A study into the importance of protective factors on desistance from violent offending for men released from custody found that intact and stable personal relationships were protective, provided those relationships were not with others involved in criminality. They also found that involvement in religious activities was a protective factor.[104]

[103] Sapouna, M., Bisset, C. and Conlong, A-M (2011) *What works to reduce reoffending: A summary of the evidence.* Justice Analytical Services, Scottish Government

[104] Coid J, Yang M, Ullrich S, Zhang T, Sizmur S, Farrington DP, et al.(2011) *Most items in structured risk assessment instruments do not predict violence.* J Forensic Psychiatry and Psychology, 22: pp.3-21

One approach that is receiving growing attention is the Good Lives Model (GLM). The model has had greater use for sex offenders than violent offenders and is used in several sex offender programmes.[105] One paper argues for the application of GLM to violent offenders, it does not include any rigorous evaluation but does usefully apply the model to a case study of a High Risk Violent Offender where it appeared to achieve some success.[106] In brief, the Good Lives Model Suggests that a number of Primary Goods are important to all human beings, including relatedness to others, connection to wider social groups, healthy living and functioning, and freedom from emotional turmoil and distress. Instrumental goods, or secondary

[105] Harkins, L., Flak, V., Beech, A.R. and Woodhams, J. (2012) *Evaluation of a community-based sex offender treatment program using a Good Lives Model approach*, Sexual Abuse: A Journal of Research and Treatment, 24, pp.519-543
[106] Whitehead, P. Ward, T. Collie, R. (2007) Time for a Change Applying the Good Lives Model of Rehabilitation to a High-Risk Violent Offender, International Journal of Offender Therapy and Comparative Criminology, 51,5, pp.578-598

goods, provide concrete means of securing primary goods and take the form of approach goals. Future oriented secondary goods, are agreed with the offender and are aimed at achieving primary goods in pro-social ways. This forms an individual plan for intervention. Dynamic risk factors are seen as obstacles to achieving the plan and so addressed at the same time. Interventions are likely to include supporting individual change with skill and capacity development and making the most of situational resources and supports.

There is some support for the view that multi-disciplinary/multi-agency approaches can be effective in work with individuals and in regulating their behaviour. In England and Wales the multi-agency assessment and management response to high risk sexual and violent offenders has been the subject of three process evaluations.[107] In brief, these evaluations focused on improving multi agency meetings, the process of information exchange, implementing risk assessment procedures, and improving risk management planning. Multi-Agency Public Protection Arrangement (MAPPA) in the UK, are 'characterised by inter-agency information sharing, risk assessment and risk management planning.[108] The authors of this paper conclude that evaluating effectiveness can be problematic, not least because of the difficulty in agreeing what constitutes an effective outcome, and differentiating between process outcomes and longer-term reductions

---

[107] Kemshall, H., Wood, J., Mackenzie, G., Bailey, R. and Yates, J. (2005) *Strengthening Multi Agency Public Protection Arrangements* (MAPPA). London: Home Office. Available at:
http://www.nhserewash.com/safeguarding/Strengthening%20MAPPA.pdf
[108] Wood, J. and Kemshall, H. (2007) *The operation and experience of Multi-Agency Public Protection Arrangements (MAPPA).*

in recidivism. A study based on a limited reconviction study comparing an offender cohort pre the introduction of MAPPA in England and Wales with a cohort post implementation found that MAPPA did contribute to recidivism reduction.[109] Whilst the study did not fully meet the requirements of a long-term reconviction study, and had some limitations in constructing fully comparable cohorts, it does represent the first evaluative study of MAPPA impact on reconviction rates for sexual and violent offenders.

Whilst a single limited study of recidivism reduction, these results are encouraging. A study in Ireland into provisions to address domestic violence recognises that multi-agency approaches are needed

---

[109] Peck, M. (2011) *Patterns of reconviction among offenders eligible for Multi-Agency Public Protection Arrangements (MAPPA)*. London: Ministry of Justice Research Series 6/11. Available at:
https://www.gov.uk/government/uploads/system/uploads/attachment_data/file/217373/patterns-reconviction-mappa.pdf

to ensure victim protection and particular issues with intimate partner violence.[110] It also recognises that coordinated approaches are essential to ensure that the range of needs of violent offenders is met. Working with others across agency borders can be facilitated through formal arrangements like MAPPA. Working together also happens in working teams made up of a range of professional disciplines co-located within a single agency, 'decision enhancing guides seem to work best when they are followed by a clinical or correctional team.'[111]

Several model programs have been described that focus on the community-based treatment of the mentally ill offender. For example, the Community Support Program was established by Wisconsin Correctional

[110] Fisher, E. (2011) *Perpetrators of Domestic Violence: Co-ordinating Responses to Complex Needs*, Irish Probation Journal, Volume 8
[111] Roehl, J. O'Sullivan, C. Webster, D. and Campbell, J. (2005) *Intimate Partner Violence Risk Assessment Validation Study*, Final Report, https://www.ncjrs.gov/pdffiles1/nij/grants/209731.pdf

Services to care for mentally ill offenders in Milwaukee, United States of America in 1978.[112] Using a "carrot and stick" approach, the program has developed five major services including medical/therapeutic services, money management, housing/other support services, day reporting/monitoring, and mandated participation. Similar in many ways to the PACT model, this program has successfully maintained a caseload averaging 250 clients/year in treatment in the community. In 1992, there were a total of 312 clients enrolled at some point during the year. During that year, 84 (27%) clients were discharged. Forty eight of these clients had completed their legal obligation, six were admitted to inpatient psychiatric services, and three to long term residential drug treatment programs. Only 15 (4.8%)

[112] McDonald DC, Teitelbaum M: *Managing Mentally Ill Offenders in the Community: Milwaukee's Community Support Program.* NIJ Program Focus, March 1994. http://www.ncjrs.org/txtfiles/ menill.txt

were arrested for new offenses or for a violation during 1992, indicating good retention and little criminal recidivism under this model.

In Multnomah County, Oregon, a number of stakeholders from the public and private sectors have come together to develop improvements in services to be delivered to the mentally disordered offender.[113] Based on a wide ranging survey of the correctional and mental health histories of a cohort of inmates, a series of guidelines were designed to address the complex, multisystem needs of this population. The council's research revealed the interesting finding that "community mental health enrollment is significantly correlated with about 12 percent lower number of jail bed days over a ten year period.[114] The

---

[113] Public Safety Coordinating Council-Report of the Work Group on the Mental Health Treatment Needs of Offenders: Severely Mentally Ill Offenders Should Be Identified and Managed By A System of Collaborating Agencies and Jurisdictions. Multnomah County, Oregon, February 7, 1997.
http://www.multnomah.lib.or.us/cc/ ds4/mental.html and subsequent linked pages.

research led to a number of recommendations regarding not only the provision of mental health and addictions services, but also regarding the key issues of housing and benefit entitlements.

The strengths of these approaches lies in their collaborative nature, with input from, participation of, and monitoring by mental health care providers and correctional officials, along with other invested parties.[115] Potential concerns include the fear that the public safety monitoring role will be thrust onto the treating clinician. In contradistinction to our work, it is important to note that neither of these programs focused specifically on paroled offenders. We describe these programs primarily to emphasize that this is a population

[114] Bureau of Justice Statistics, United States Department of Justice, Corrections facts at a glance, revision dated May 27, 1997, http://www.ojp.usdoj.gov/bjs/glance/corr2.txt. Interdisciplinary Teams and Supportive Services. Multnomah County, Oregon, February 7, 1997. http://www.multnomah.lib.or.us/cc/ ds4/inter.html.
[115] Prins H: *The Care of the Psychiatric Prisoner-Discharge into the Community and Its Implications. Medicine*, Science and the Law 23(2):79-86, 1983.

that can be treated successfully if we utilize appropriate models of care.

The two programs described above underscore the need for correctional and mental health personnel to work collaboratively with this difficult population. Also, although incarcerated males make up more of the prison population than incarcerated females, a greater percentage of female inmates are mentally ill.[116] According to a report by the Bureau of Justice Statistics (which uses computer-assisted personal interviewing), 11% of female inmates report mental illness as compared to only 6% of male inmates.[117] However, another source claims that one third to two thirds of female inmates need mental-

[116] Ditton, P. M. (1999). *Mental health and treatment of inmates and probationers*, (NCJ No. 174463). Washington, DC: Office of Justice Programs, Bureau of Justice Statistics, U.S. Department of Justice. Retrieved from http://bjs.ojp.usdoj.gov/index.cfm?ty=pbdetail&iid=787

[117] Maruschak, L. M. (2004). *Medical problems of prisoners* (NCJ No. 221740). Washington, DC: Office of Justice Programs, Bureau of Justice Statistics, U.S. Department of Justice. Retrieved from http://bjs.ojp.usdoj.gov/index.cfm?ty=pbdetail&iid=1097

health services.[118]   A   partial explanation for these differences is that the criminal justice system, as will be discussed later, can put a lot of stress on inmates. The new environment, along with the increased stress, can cause depression and anxiety, among other things, to develop. Therefore, women who weren't mentally ill before entering the criminal justice system may need to utilize the mental health services avail-able. Also, female inmates, as opposed to male inmates, were more likely to report receiving treatment,[119] which is a trend supported by research.

Based on surveys of patients in a mental health clinic, it was found that women had more positive attitudes towards treatment, and are thus

[118] Soderstrom, I. A. (2007). *Mental illness in offender populations: Prevalence, duty and implications.* Journal of Offender Rehabilitation, 45, 1–17. doi:10.1300/J076v45n01_01

[119] Ditton, P. M. (1999). *Mental health and treatment of inmates and probationers,* (NCJ No. 174463). Washington, DC: Office of Justice Programs, Bureau of Justice Statistics, U.S. Department of Justice. Retrieved from http://bjs.ojp.usdoj.gov/index.cfm?ty=pbdetail&iid=787

more likely than men to seek mental health treatment and use mental health ser-vices that are available to them.[120] SAMHSA[121] also found similar results in their National Survey on Drug Use and Health. Women were more likely to use professional mental health services than men, 17% compared to 9%. Although this may partially account for the difference, it is also possible that more females than males in the criminal justice system experience mental illness.

Although African Americans and Hispanics are overrepresented in the prison population, Caucasian inmates are more likely to report having a mental illness than African American or Hispanic

[120] Elhai, J. D., Patrick, S. L., Anderson, S., Simons, J. S., & Frueh, B. C. (2006). *Gender- and trauma-related predictors of use of mental health treatment services among primary care patient.* Psychiatric Services, 57, 1505–1509. doi:10.1176/appi.ps.57.10.1505

[121] Substance Abuse and Mental Health Services Administration. (2010). *Results from the 2009 national survey on drug use and health*: Mental health findings (Office of Applied Studies, NSDUH Series H-39, HHS Publication No. SMA 10-4609). Retrieved from http://oas.samhsa.gov/nsduh/2k9nsduh/2k9resultsp.pdf

inmates .[122] A 2005 report stated that 12% of African American males ages 25–29 were in the criminal justice system, compared to 3.7% of Hispanic males of the same age group, and 1.7% of Caucasian male equivalents.[123] In 2005, the Bureau of Justice Statistics estimated that 61% of Caucasian inmates report any mental health problem as compared to 54% of African American inmates and 44% of Hispanic inmates.[124]

Whether or not the correctional system is the proper place for the mentally ill, their presence there creates a number of treatment problems. Due to limited resources such as time, space, and money, the

[122] O'Keefe, M. L., & Schnell, M. J. (2007). *Offenders with mental illness in the correctional system.* Journal of Offender Rehabilitation, 45, 81–104. doi:10.1300/J076v45n01_08

[123] Harrison, P. M., & Beck, A. J. (2006). *Prison and jail inmates at midyear 2005* (NCJ No. 213133). Washington, DC: Office of Justice Programs, Bureau of Justice Statistics, U.S. Department of Justice. Retrieved from http://bjs.ojp.usdoj.gov/index.cfm?ty=pbdetail&iid=1007

[124] James, D. J., & Glaze, L. E. (2006). *Mental health problems of prison and jail inmates* (NCJ No. 213600). Washington, DC: Office of Justice Programs, Bureau of Justice Statistics, U.S. Department of Justice. Retrieved from http://bjs.ojp.usdoj.gov/index.cfm?ty=pbdetail&iid=789

most common form treatment given to mentally ill inmates is the administering of medications.[125] We cannot be sure whether medication is used to treat the mental illness or to control the symptoms of the illness to make it easier for correctional staff and administration. Correctional staff are only able to assess inmates, provide crisis management, and monitor inmates' medications.[126] Worse yet, less than half of mentally ill inmates receive any form of treatment.[127] Correctional staff are not trained to handle mentally ill inmates, which creates another treatment problem. Correctional staff are in the best position to watch for symptoms of a mental illness, but most are not trained to do so.

[125] Adams, K., & Ferrandino, J. (2008). *Managing mentally ill inmates in prisons*. Criminal Justice and Behavior, 35, 913–927. doi:10.1177/0093854808318624

[126] O'Keefe, M. L. (2007). *Administrative segregation for mentally ill inmates*. Journal of Offender Rehabilitation, 45, 149–165. doi:10.1300/J076v45n01_11

[127] James, D. J., & Glaze, L. E. (2006). *Mental health problems of prison and jail inmates* (NCJ No. 213600). Washington, DC: Office of Justice Programs, Bureau of Justice Statistics, U.S. Department of Justice. Retrieved from http://bjs.ojp.usdoj.gov/index.cfm?ty=pbdetail&iid=789

Therefore, inmates may not receive the care they deserve and require.[128] However, based on a survey of jail administrators, participants indicated that one of the most effective interventions was mental health training for staff, but it is unclear to what extent this is being used.[129] Correctional officers who do recognize the symptoms of mental illness and do not act may have doubts about the psychological explanations of behavior or may refrain from acting due to a lack of resources.[130] Although providing medication is the one form of treatment that correctional officers take part in, they are not trained to do so.[131] Correctional staff experience

[128] Phillips, D. W. (2005). *Mentally ill people and the criminal justice system.* Criminal Justice Review, 30, 215–219. doi:10.1177/0734016805282751

[129] Ruddell, R. (2006). *Jail interventions for inmates with mental illnesses.* Journal of Correctional Health Care, 12, 118–131. doi:10.1177/1078345806288957

[130] Rhodes, L. A. (2005). *Pathological effects of the supermaximum prison.* American Journal of Public Health, 95, 1692–1695. doi:10.2105/AJPH.2005.070045

[131] Turner, C. (2007). *Ethical issues in criminal justice administration.* American Jails, 20, 49–53.

the conflicting roles of controlling and maintaining safety, and providing treatment.[132] The resulting cognitive dissonance, unless addressed and resolved in some sort of training, would result in the correctional officer fulfilling only one of those roles. It would seem that the default role the correctional staff would fulfill would be the role of controlling and maintaining safety due to the lack of training concerning treatment. The same dissonance that individual officers confront, the conflict between treating and managing inmates, characterizes the correctional system itself. Mental health professionals and correctional staff operate independently of one another and often have hostile relationships and conflicting roles.[133]

[132] Adams, K., & Ferrandino, J. (2008). *Managing mentally ill inmates in prisons*. Criminal Justice and Behavior, 35, 913–927. doi:10.1177/0093854808318624

[133] Soderstrom, I. A. (2007). *Mental illness in offender populations: Prevalence, duty and implications*. Journal of Offender Rehabilitation, 45, 1–17. doi:10.1300/J076v45n01_01

Mental health professionals focus on diagnosing and treating, whereas correctional staff and administration focus on management and the safety of inmates.[134] Administrators often place the treatment needs of mentally ill inmates after maintaining security and control in the correctional system.[135] The correctional environment can be difficult for mentally ill inmates because of the rules and regulations of prisons. An examination of the in-facility offenses of inmates in the Colorado Department of Corrections found that mentally ill inmates had a higher rate of disciplinary actions than the general population, and because of the number of violations were more likely to be placed in higher security units, such

[134] Geraghty, T. F., & Kraus, L. J. (1998). *Treating the mentally-ill offender: The chal-lenges of creating an effective, safe and just system.* Journal of Criminal Law & Criminology, 89, 393–402.
[135] O'Keefe, M. L., & Schnell, M. J. (2007). *Offenders with mental illness in the correctional system.* Journal of Offender Rehabilitation, 45, 81–104. doi:10.1300/J076v45n01_08

as administrative segregation.[136] Another study found that mentally ill inmates were charged with rule violations at a higher rate than non mentally ill inmates, including 58% compared to 43% in state prisons, 40% compared to 28% in federal prisons, and 19% compared to 9% in jails.[137] Rule violations, both violent and nonviolent, are more common in offenders with depression and psychosis, as well as in those who experience hopelessness, paranoia, and hallucinations.[138] Many mentally ill inmates are not able to understand the rules and regulations of prisons and therefore suffer the consequences of breaking the rules.[139] Because of

[136] O'Keefe, M. L. (2007). *Administrative segregation for mentally ill inmates.* Journal of Offender Rehabilitation, 45, 149–165. doi:10.1300/J076v45n01_11

[137] James, D. J., & Glaze, L. E. (2006). *Mental health problems of prison and jail inmates* (NCJ No. 213600). Washington, DC: Office of Justice Programs, Bureau of Justice Statistics, U.S. Department of Justice. Retrieved from http://bjs.ojp.usdoj.gov/index.cfm?ty=pbdetail&iid=789

[138] Felson, R. B., Silver, E., & Remster, B. (2012). *Mental disorder and offending in prison.* Criminal Justice and Behavior, 39, 125–143. doi:10.1177/0093854811428565

[139] Geiman, D. (2007). *Confronting the challenge with training: Managing inmates with mental health disorders.* Corrections Today, 69, 22–23.

manifestations of their ill-nesses, illogical thinking, and the effects of isolation, mentally ill inmates often are not able to understand the rules. Because administrators and correctional staff are more focused on security, control, and management, rule violations often cause mentally ill inmates to end up being punished for things they don't understand and may be placed in administrative segregation. The inappropriate use of administrative segregation—isolation, maxi-mum security, and super maximum security facilities creates another problem in the treatment of the mentally ill. Administrative segregation is usually reserved for inmates who pose the greatest threat to the security of the prison or in some cases, to protect mentally ill inmates from the general inmate population. James and Glaze (2006) found that mentally ill inmates were injured more than twice the rate as non-mentally ill inmates, suggesting that they are victimized among the general population. A survey of inmates evaluating the rates of victimization in prison revealed that male inmates with mental disorders were physically victimized 1.6 times more often by other inmates and 1.2 times more often by staff, and female inmates with mental disorders were 1.7 times more likely to be victimized by other inmates, with no difference in terms of staff victimization.[140] Administrative segregation is also used to control behavior that is a manifestation of the illness because of the lack of space in psychiatric facilities.[141] While this is the cheapest way to deal with

[140] Blitz, C. L., Wolff, N., & Shi, J. (2008). *Physical victimization in prison: The role of mental illness.* International Journal of Law and Psychiatry, 31, 385–393. doi:10.1016/j.ijlp.2008.08.005
[141] Rhodes, L. A. (2005). *Pathological effects of the supermaximum prison.* American Journal of Public Health, 95, 1692–1695. doi:10.2105/AJPH.2005.070045

mentally ill inmates, this can often lead to an increased risk of suicide. When correctional officers recognized an increased risk of suicide, they strip and isolate the inmates in order to protect them. This can be seen as punishment to mentally ill inmates, which often leads them to keep suicidal thoughts and behaviors hidden.[142] Inmates who are "disturbed and disruptive" are often sent to administrative segregation because they are the inmates who are more likely to break rules than other non mentally ill inmates.[143] These inmates most likely have some form of mental illness. Some of the manifestations of their illnesses that make them disturbed and disruptive could be controlled by medication, but often medication is not received and in order to control

[142] Adams, K., & Ferrandino, J. (2008). *Managing mentally ill inmates in prisons.* Criminal Justice and Behavior, 35, 913–927. doi:10.1177/0093854808318624

[143] Hodgins, S., & Cote, G. (1991). *The mental health of penitentiary inmates in isolation.* Canadian Journal of Criminology, 33, 175–182

them; as a result, mentally ill inmates are put in administrative segregation. A lack of mental health resources for inmates results in an overrepresentation of mentally ill inmates in administrative segregation.[144] Segregation can have very harmful effects on all inmates, but especially on the mentally ill. Even though segregation can exacerbate mental illness, correctional facilities often use segregation as a way of dealing with mentally ill inmates.[145] Severe mental illnesses, such as schizophrenia and bipolar disorder, are more prevalent in segregation than in the general prison population. Although administrative segregation can be used to control and protect mentally ill inmates, it does not allow them the same access to the

[144] Soderstrom, I. A. (2007). *Mental illness in offender populations: Prevalence, duty and implications*. Journal of Offender Rehabilitation, 45, 1–17. doi:10.1300/J076v45n01_01

[145] Hodgins, S., & Cote, G. (1991). *The mental health of penitentiary inmates in isolation*. Canadian Journal of Criminology, 33, 175–182

programs and ser-vices that are available to the general inmate population.[146] Many treatment programs do not address co-occurring disorders and the failure to do so is another problem in the treatment of the mentally ill in corrections. Treatment, if received at all, is focused on a single diagnosis. Because many mentally ill inmates also have co-occurring disorders, often substance abuse disorders, treating only one diagnosis can pose a problem when it comes to the treatment and care that mentally ill inmates receive. Usually the disorder that does get treated, if it is addressed at all, is the most prominent disorder that produces the most disruptive behavior. Because the main focus of correction environments is to control, they focus only on the disorder that causes most

[146] O'Keefe, M. L., & Schnell, M. J. (2007). *Offenders with mental illness in the correctional system*. Journal of Offender Rehabilitation, 45, 81–104. doi:10.1300/J076v45n01_08

of the problems. However, if co-occurring disorders are not treated, the treatment of mental illnesses will likely not be effective long term. This poses a problem, because an untreated disorder can often lead to recidivism.[147] Correctional facilities often have inadequate resources in order to be able to provide the proper care that mentally ill inmates need. One study found that inmates with mental illness had greater needs than the general population, in areas including academic, vocational, substance abuse, medical, anger, and self-destruction.[148] According to a census of state and federal facilities, most facilities (95%) claim to provide mental health services.[149] The most common service is a mental-health

[147] Knoll, J. (2006). *A tale of two crises: Mental health treatment in corrections.* Journal of Dual Diagnosis, 3, 7–21. doi:10.1300/J374v03n01_03

[148] O'Keefe, M. L., & Schnell, M. J. (2007). *Offenders with mental illness in the correctional system.* Journal of Offender Rehabilitation, 45, 81–104. doi:10.1300/J076v45n01_08

[149] Beck, A. J., & Maruschak (2001). *Mental health treatment in state prisons, 2000* (NCJ No. 188215). Washington, DC: Office of Justice Programs, Bureau of Justice Statistics, U.S. Department of Justice. Retrieved from http://bjs.ojp.usdoj.gov/index.cfm?ty=pbdetail&iid=788

intake screening, with 70% of all state and federal facilities using this method. While 51% of state prisons provide 24-hour mental care only 10% of mentally ill inmates received 24-hour care. Mental health services are more likely in higher security facilities, leaving some minimum and medium security facilities without the appropriate services. These numbers do not represent a level of adequate, available treatment for mentally ill inmates. Even though most facilities use an intake screening, they may not be effective enough at detecting mental illness. Based on the data of offenders in Colorado's Department of Corrections and semi-structured interviews, O'Keefe and Schnell (2007) found that mental illness detected at admissions remained relatively stable over a 5-year period, how-ever, mental illness in the correctional population increased over the same period. This suggests that intake tools may not be sufficient in identifying offenders with mental illness, or that symptoms of mental illness appear after admission, suggestion an effect of the environment on the mental health of inmates. The prison environment will be discussed at more length later, but the issue of adequacy of intake screening measures provides a potential case in which the criminal justice system could use improvement. Another study found that while 96% of jails surveyed in one state screened inmates at admission, none of the jails used an evidence-based screening tool, and most asked only vague questions about general health.[150] Only 5% of the jails asked specific questions about mental illness, again indicating that improvement is needed in this area. The most common form of treatment for

[150] Scheyett, A., Vaughn, J., & Taylor, M. F. (2009). *Screening and access to services for individuals with serious mental illness in jails.* Community Mental Health Journal, 45, 439–446. doi:10.1007/s10597-009-9204-9

mentally ill inmates is that of the distribution of medication.[151] Medication alone is not adequate treatment. Medication should be coupled with therapy and/or counseling. A 2000 Census of State and Federal Adult Correctional Facilities found that 73% of facilities distribute medication to approximately 10% of the inmate population, with some facilities distributing to less than five percent and some up to 20%.[152] Given that approximately 16% of inmates are mentally ill, and that other inmates likely have medical conditions for which they receive medication, medication is likely not being used as much as it could be. Although some prisons contain specially designed mental health units, the high cost

[151] Adams, K., & Ferrandino, J. (2008). *Managing mentally ill inmates in prisons.* Criminal Justice and Behavior, 35, 913–927. doi:10.1177/0093854808318624

[152] Beck, A. J., & Maruschak (2001). *Mental health treatment in state prisons, 2000* (NCJ No. 188215). Washington, DC: Office of Justice Programs, Bureau of Justice Statistics, U.S. Department of Justice. Retrieved from http://bjs.ojp.usdoj.gov/index.cfm?ty=pbdetail&iid=788

and limited space of these units prevents many mentally ill inmates from being placed there and are rather placed in the general prison population where they do not receive the treatment they need.[153] Some prisons have treatment groups, but due to limited staff and resources, there is limited availability and variability of programs, which results in some mentally ill inmates not being, placed in these treatment groups. Bewley and Morgan (2011) interviewed mental health service providers from state correctional facilities, most of whom were psychologists (58%), about the mental health services available to inmates with mental illness. The researchers found that the majority, 57%, had received no specific training in correctional or forensic psychology, and only a quarter had completed

[153] O'Keefe, M. L., & Schnell, M. J. (2007). *Offenders with mental illness in the correctional system*. Journal of Offender Rehabilitation, 45, 81–104. doi:10.1300/J076v45n01_08

either any courses in correctional psychology, a correctional practicum, or a correctional internship. The participants estimated that 23% of the offender population is mentally ill, but 27% of all offenders receive mental health services. Although half of participants agreed that rehabilitation was an important goal in their prison, 65% were dissatisfied about lack of necessary funding. In regards to the treatment that was being provided, participants rated their effectiveness between "neutral" and "mildly effective." Although a form of treatment known as "risk need responsivity" is a widely accepted and comprehensive theory, it was not one of the main areas of concern for providers, which the researchers suggest is evidence that mental health service providers are not focusing on offender treatment literature. While vocational training is significant in preventing recidivism, only 16% of facilities offered such training. According to the Bureau of Justice Statistics, 34% of mentally ill inmates in state prisons and 17% in jails report having received treatment since arrival. Although medication received by all state inmates increased from 1997 to 2004, the rates of medication use for mentally ill inmates are still quite low, as are other treatment methods. This includes 27% medication, 22% counseling, and 5% overnight hospital stay for prisons and 15% medication, 7% counseling, and 2% overnight hospital stay for jails. The Bureau based its estimates on personal interviews and inmate data. Another source claims that based on a nationwide governmental study, 79% of men-tally ill inmates receive mental health treatment in the form of therapy or counseling from a professional on a regular basis.[154]

[154] Beck, A. J., & Maruschak (2001). *Mental health treatment in state prisons, 2000* (NCJ No. 188215). Washington, DC: Office of Justice Programs,

Even if this higher estimate is more accurate, this still leaves 21% of mentally ill inmates untreated. It may be that the 21% that goes untreated refuses treatment, or that there are not adequate resources to treat all of mentally ill inmates. Even those who do receive treatment may not receive the best treatment available. With a limited number of treatment professionals, each professional has more patients, decreasing his or her effectiveness.[155] The prison environment creates psychological effects on all inmates, but these effects can be even greater in mentally ill inmates. In segregation, mentally ill inmates have more severe psychopathology, which may be an effect of the environment, and higher activity and lower impulse control, which may explain why the

Bureau of Justice Statistics, U.S. Department of Justice. Retrieved from http://bjs.ojp.usdoj.gov/index.cfm?ty=pbdetail&iid=788
[155] O'Keefe, M. L., & Schnell, M. J. (2007). *Offenders with mental illness in the correctional system*. Journal of Offender Rehabilitation, 45, 81–104. doi:10.1300/J076v45n01_08

inmates were placed in segregation in the first place.[156] After mentally ill inmates are released from segregation, perceptual changes, affective disturbances, cognitive problems, disturbing thoughts and lack of impulse control can be seen as well as other psycho-logical symptoms such as increased anxiety, headaches, nervous breakdowns, and lethargy. Psychosocial problems such as social withdrawal and irrational anger are also present. The prison environment destroys autonomy, self-initiative, and can damage long-term psychological health.[157] Administrative segregation is often a concentrated representation of all the negative effects of a prison environment,[158] and mentally ill inmates are often placed there

[156] O'Keefe, M. L. (2007). *Administrative segregation for mentally ill inmates.* Journal of Offender Rehabilitation, 45, 149–165. doi:10.1300/J076v45n01_11

[157] Knoll, J. (2006). *A tale of two crises: Mental health treatment in corrections.* Journal of Dual Diagnosis, 3, 7–21. doi:10.1300/J374v03n01_03

[158] Rhodes, L. A. (2005). *Pathological effects of the supermaximum prison.* American Journal of Public Health, 95, 1692–1695. doi:10.2105/AJPH.2005.070045

making it more likely that they come out of prisons with more problems than when they went in. The effects of imprisonment on mentally ill inmates, especially when they are placed in isolation or in an overcrowded environment, often create an increased risk for self-injury and suicide. A psychiatrist's estimate of the number of unsuccessful suicide attempts to successful suicide attempts was 20 to 1 (Turner, 2007). Suicide is especially common in mentally ill inmates, particularly when mental illness goes untreated. Often, treatment is not received until a mental illness has gotten worse. Many times, mentally ill inmates have to exaggerate their illness in order to be recognized and receive treatment. SAMHSA (2010) found that adults on probation in the previous year were more than twice as likely than the general population to have a serious mental illness, and adults on parole or supervised release were also more likely to experience serious mental illness, 11.8 % and 9.7%, respectively, compared to 4.8% in the general population. This suggests that experiences in the criminal justice system may facilitate the development of a serious mental illness. Because of the inadequate care received and the effects of imprisonment, problems faced by mentally ill inmates in corrections include rehabilitation, recidivism, and offender reentry. Although some claim that no relationship exists between mental illness and recidivism,[159] others disagree. Based on personal interviews, the Bureau of Justice Statistics estimates that over 75% of the mentally ill inmate population had at least one prior sentence.[160]

---

[159] Lamberti, J. S. (2007). *Understanding and preventing criminal recidivism among adults with psychotic disorders*. Psychiatric Services, 58, 773–781. doi:10.1176/appi.ps.58.6.773

[160] Ditton, P. M. (1999). *Mental health and treatment of inmates and probationers* (NCJ No. 174463). Washington, DC: Office of Justice Programs, Bureau of

Half of all mentally ill inmates had three or more prior sentences and 10% had eleven or more offenses as compared to 5% of other inmates. This suggests that mentally ill inmates have a potentially high recidivism rate, potentially due to public order arrests and lack of community resources. Also, mentally ill inmates were more likely to be violent recidivists (53%) than the general prison population (45%). Inmates with serious mental illness are more likely to have previous incarcerations, especially those with bipolar disorder.[161] Inmates placed in administrative segregation were more likely than non-segregated inmates to re-offend. Psychosis itself is a risk factor for offender recidivism. Potential causes of this high

Justice Statistics, U.S. Department of Justice. Retrieved from http://bjs.ojp.usdoj.gov/index.cfm?ty=pbdetail&iid=787

[161] Baillargeon, J., Binswanger, I. A., Penn, J. V., Williams, B. A., & Murray, O. J. (2009). *Psychiatric disorders and repeat incarcerations: The revolving prison door.* American Journal of Psychiatry, 166, 103–109. doi:10.1176/appi.ajp.2008.08030416

recidivism rate are inadequate treatment and co-occurring disorders. With adequate treatment and if all disorders were addressed, it is likely that we would be able to reduce mentally ill inmate recidivism. Another potential cause of the high recidivism rate among inmates with mental illness is a lack of personal and community assets. Mentally ill inmates were also more than 2 times as likely as other inmates to have been homeless in the year before their arrest and more likely than other inmates to have been unemployed before their arrest.[162] Greenberg and Rosenheck (2008) suggested that the strong association between homeless-ness and mental illness among inmates may be caused by the lack of mental health services in the community,

[162] Greenberg, G. A., & Rosenheck, R. A. (2008). *Jail incarceration, homelessness, and mental health: A national study.* Psychiatric Services, 59,170–177. doi:10.1176/appi.ps.59.2.170

deinstitutionalization, legal restrictions on involuntary commitment, and the limited knowledge of mental health issues by police. For all inmates, rehabilitation is not usually the focus of their incarceration. Our society has become more interested in punishing criminals instead of rehabilitating them.[163] Prison itself is an environment that does not make rehabilitation easy, especially for mentally ill inmates. Because so many mentally ill inmates are placed in administrative segregation, they become exceedingly dependent on others, usually correctional officers, and they lose any social skills, self-control, and self-management. This makes it hard for mentally ill, upon release, to rejoin society as independent adults. Mentally ill inmates are more likely than inmates

[163] Knoll, J. (2006). *A tale of two crises: Mental health treatment in corrections.* Journal of Dual Diagnosis, 3, 7–21. doi:10.1300/J374v03n01_03

without mental illness to be released into the community right out of administrative segregation and are less likely to be placed in a transitional halfway house, which helps offenders rejoin and become productive members of society. Because the prison environment is so focused on punishment, especially in administrative segregation, inmates may develop a punitive attitude that will eventually affect their family and community upon release.

These are just some methods which have been proposed by various scholars which all suggest that there is a possibility that through rehabilitation there is a scope of reducing recidivism. There is only so much detail about it because much of this has been limited to academic teaching and has not been applied and tested in a lot many places. Although one thing common amongst all the places where rehabilitation is considered for offenders, and that is that all these countries are considered as 'Developed Countries' by all means may it be socially, economically, or any parameter there may be. So if the country has to make the next step from being a developing country to a developed country it has to take the steps necessary to achieve that goal, and ethical treatment of all people is a very important aspect of a country in determining what form of society exists in that particular part of the world.

Chapter 4: Norway shows how to do it the right way!

A successful prison system is where one is reformed in a manner that he does not intend to commit any crime once being released from there. A low recidivism rate, rather a declining recidivism rate should be the primary parameter to decide the efficiency of a prison system. Norway has been one of the few countries to have achieved this objective of reducing recidivism and today the prison system in Norway is an example for all the developed and developing countries. It is referred as the world's most humane prison system. Kriminalomsorgen, Norway's correctional system, focuses on rehabilitation and reintegration into the society as the primary purpose of prison and implements these policies through Principles of Normality, which states that the life of an inmate at prison should be as similar as possible to outside prison.

The citizens of Norway believe that the sole punishment of prison should be limited to loss of liberty, and that the offenders should continue to be entitled to all other legal rights and services to that of any other ordinary citizen. Bastoy Prison and Halden Prison stand out as two of Norway's most talked-of prisons, famous for its luxurious amenities and services. Tranquility does not come cheaply. A place at Halden Prison costs about £98,000 per year.[164] As per the NCRB annual reports, the annual expenditure per inmate on various heads like food, clothing, medical, vocational/educational & other welfare activities has been on the rise. The average expenditure per inmate has gone up from Rs. 19447 in 2010-11 to Rs. 29538 in 2014-15. This is an increase of over 50% in five years.[165]

---

[164] *How Norway turns criminals into good neighbours*, BBC Stories, 6 July,2019, accessed from https://www.bbc.com/news/stories-48885846 on 29.12.2020

Kriminalomsorgen manages Norway's prisons and the custody of its inmates with the objective of keeping its citizens safe and reducing recidivism by allowing offenders to improve their character through their own efforts and initiatives. Norway relies on restorative justice, which focuses on rehabilitation and repairing the harm caused by the crime rather than simply punishing the offender. Kriminalomsorgen makes efforts to resolve crimes while considering the interests of the offender, victims, family and friends, and community at large. The Principle of Normality guides the Norwegian corrections system. As discussed this guiding principle states that the punishment for the crime is only the restriction of liberty. The sentenced offender does not lose its other rights and has all of the other rights that

---

[165] Rakesh Dubbudu, *Expenditure per Prison inmate increased by over 50% in 5 years*, Factly, June 20, 2016, accessed from https://factly.in/expenditure-per-prison-inmate-increased-50-5-years/ on 29.12.2020

Norwegian citizens are entitled to outside of the corrections system. Norwegian prisoners retain their right to study and their right to vote. The Principle of Normality dictates that life inside prison while serving a sentence must resemble life outside of prison as much as possible. Thus, no one will serve their prison sentence under stricter conditions than is necessary to ensure the safety of the outside citizens, and offenders must be placed in the lowest feasible security regimen. Norwegians justify this principle with the argument that the more closed off a prison system is, the harder it will be for the offender to reintegrate into the community at the end of his sentencing period when released. The motto of Kriminalomsorgen is "better out than in"[166] and the agency collaborates with other government

[166] Jessica Benko, *The Radical Humaneness of Norway's Halden Prisont.*, March 26,2015, The New York Times Magazine accessed from https://www.nytimes.com/2015/03/29/magazine/the-radical-humaneness-of-norways-halden-prison.html on 27.12.2020

agencies to ensure that the inmate has housing, employment and a supportive social network available upon release.

The aim of the system as the offender progresses through his sentence is to prepare him as much as possible for return to the community. This is especially important in Norway where the longest prison sentence that can be given is 21 years which is very similar to that of India's life sentence period although Norway does not have the provisions for lifetime imprisonment and death penalty with a couple of very rare exceptions. A sentence of 30 years can be given for atrocities or wrongdoings against humankind, and especially risky guilty parties can be assigned to preventive detention in addition to their sentence. Preventive confinement is just considered for perilous, rational guilty parties where a conventional time-restricted sentence is considered lacking to guarantee the network's wellbeing. Wrongdoers condemned to preventive detainment have submitted an offense that is hurtful to another's life, wellbeing, or opportunity and are considered by the appointed authority to have a generous probability of re-offending later on. Preventive detainment requires the judge to inspect the wrongdoer toward the finish of the assigned jail sentence to check whether he still poses a huge danger to the network for re-offending. On the off chance that the appropriate response is yes, at that point the sentence is extended by five years. The assessment at that point happens again after the extra fiveyears and can possibly proceed indefinitely to result in a lifelong incarceration. Notwithstanding, Kriminalomsorgen is obligated to work with the wrongdoer towards recovery so the danger might be diminished and the guilty party can be eliminated from preventive detainment. Norway at present has only 94 people in preventive confinement including Anders Breivik, the scandalous racial oppressor who murdered 77peoplevia shooting and bombing, with a significant number of the casualties being children. To date, the longest anybody has ever served in Norway under preventive detainment is 30 years. The normal jail sentence in Norway is only eight months in length. In reality, over 60% of jail sentences are three months or less and practically 90% of jail sentences are short of what one year. Thus, the dominant part of wrongdoers in the Norwegian jail framework will be delivered from jail in a moderately brief timeframe, so reintegration into the network is vital. The Norwegian people believe that the more shut off a jail framework is, the more unlikely will be the successful return to the network. As a feature of the cycle of reintegration, wrongdoers move from high security jails to bring down security detainment facilities and afterward asylums as they close to the furthest limit of their terms.

Likewise in line with reintegration is the import model used by Kriminalomsorgen. The import model directs that neighborhood and metropolitan suppliers convey fundamental administrations straightforwardly to the detainment facilities. This implies nearby organizations and associations from the network go to the jail to offer clinical, instructive, library, administrative, and business administrations to the detainees. These administrations are financed by the state at no expense to the detainees since they are ensured privileges of all occupants of Norway. The import model endeavors to make a consistent way, which means the wrongdoer has a place with a similar region when his jail sentence. As expressed before, the solitary right lost by the wrongdoers is their freedom, and they hold any remaining rights. This contribution of administrations by the public makes the network more associated with the wrongdoers, permitting the guilty parties to set up contact and associations with those external jail. At the point when the wrongdoers are delivered once again into the network they will have an important organization—for employment and different necessities—that will permit them to more readily reintegrate into society and abstain from recidivating. Norway has extremely low populace thickness with a weird shape that is long and limited. This phenomenon is compounded by the way that Norway puts a substantial accentuation on having its detainees serve their time close to their homes to advance recovery and reintegration through simple admittance to their informal community and nearby specialist organizations. To tackle this issue, Norway has numerous little prisons. Norway's jail limit is only 3,900 cells, yet thesecellsare spread across 43 detainment facilities in 61 areas. Norway's biggest jail is situated in its capital, Oslo, which has 392 cells. The normal Norwegian jail has only 70 cells, and the littlest just 13. Not at all like the prison framework in the United States, Norway has no different pre-preliminary confinement habitats.

Norway carefully submits to a one man for every cell policyin request to guarantee humandignity. This approach has caused a few issues sincethe country's jail limit is only 3,900, and there are not in every case enough cells for condemned people. In this way, the framework uses a holding up rundown. Under this framework, when limit is pushed to the limit, condemned wrongdoers approach their lives as regular on transitory leave until they get a letter advising them that a space has opened. At that point the guilty party should answer to the specified facility to finish his sentence. Since jail sentences are so short, wrongdoers never stay on this rundown for over one year. Over 99% of detainees on impermanent leave return on an ideal opportunity to carry out their punishments. In any case, endeavors were taken to lessen the holding up rundown by 25% of its length, so less wrongdoers would need to stand by to finish their sentences.In actuality, the framework is as of now running at under full capacity.

Prison officials in Norway go through a broad two-year instruction program at the Staff Academy. The authority set of working responsibilities of these jail officials expects them to "spur the detainee with the goal that his sentence is as important, illuminating, and restoring as could reasonably be expected." During this preparation period, the officials get full compensation and are shown brain science, criminology, morals, law, and basic freedoms. About 40% of all Norwegian jail officials are female, and none of the officials are furnished. This is with regards to Norwegian law denying its police power from conveying guns without uncommon approval. Norwegian officials depend on powerful security, as opposed to static security employed elsewhere in the world. Static security is intended to keep detainees with terrible goals from helping them out through methods, for example, far off controlled entryways, shackles, restricted association, and sealed furnishings. In the interim, unique security centers around keeping awful expectations from framing in any case, and Norway achieves this through creating connections between the officials and prisoners. The officials and detainees are regularly nearby other people with one another, and frequently mingle together. Each Norwegian detainee is matched with his own contact-official. The contact-official is answerable for helping the detainee to effectively finish his sentence by keeping up his contacts with outside outsiders and service suppliers, also as officials inside the jail framework. The contact-official will likewise help the detainee round out applications to be moved to a lower security jail, answer examines the prisoner has concerning jail, and consistently catch up with the prisoner to perceive how he is adapting and progressing.

Kriminalomsorgen has four diverse security levels for its penitentiaries:

extra-high security, high-security, low-security, and temporary lodging. Then again, prisoners may serve their time in different foundations in the event that they require mental consideration or restoration for drug abuse. The extra-high security level is genuinely new, as it was presented in 2002. Additional high-security is utilized particularly rarely, as only 15 prisoners have been held under extra-high security since its creation, including Anders Breivik. Further, detainees may just be held in additional high-security for as long as 21 months prior to being moved to a lower security level. Almost 66% of guilty parties start their sentences at high-security penitentiaries prior to being moved to bring down security detainment facilities. High-security detainment facilities have a fence around the jail, and detainees are secured their cells around evening time. Guilty parties in high-security jails have private cells with their own latrine, sink, and TV. Low-security detainment facilities have less wellbeing measures. 36% of Norway's penitentiaries are named low-security, and they offer advantages, for example, limitless calls and as long as four days of leave for each month. Low-security detainment facilities may or may not have a fence around the jail, and detainees are not secured cells around evening time. Undoubtedly, detainees at low-security jails frequently share houses with different prisoners where they each have their own rooms. Momentary lodging, or asylums, are the least level in the jail framework, and most of Norway's wrongdoers finish their sentences in temporary lodging. The essential target of momentary lodging is for the detainee to get and start a line of work outside of the jail framework. Detainees are permitted to look for a work themselves, or may look for the help of Kriminalomsorgen. Momentary lodging likewise centers around making sure about the wrongdoer's future lodging and social requirements.

Kriminalomsorgen additionally uses a probation, or delivery on permit, framework. Likewise to the jails, the probation workplaces are various and spread out with 17 workplaces in 40 locations across the nation to more readily help wrongdoers. These probation workplaces are answerable for guaranteeing that non-jail sentences—which are used much of the time by the courts—are finished. These people group sanctions incorporate home detainment with or without electronic checking, discharge on permit, and the program against inebriated driving. A people group sentence can last somewhere in the range of 30 and 420 hours, which is a greatest of17.5 days. Network sentences involve work and different exercises specifically aimed at keeping the guilty party from reoffending. Thus, most detainees start their sentences in a high-security jail prior to being moved to a low-security jail lastly completing their sentences in a shelter, which allows for the continuous exchange from jail to full opportunity. In reality, numerous prisoners are even permitted to take "breaks" from their sentences, during which they are permitted to make trips home to see loved ones.

The period of criminal duty in Norway is 15 years of age. In any case, it is government strategy that nobody younger than 18 ought to be detained. Just adolescents between the ages of 15 and 18 that submit the most genuine offenses will be dependent upon detainment, and there are right now not many young people under 18 spending time in jail in Norwegian penitentiaries. For these uncommon cases, two unique organizations have been explicitly worked to house adolescent wrongdoers, and they employ extensive rehabilitative estimates such as high staff to detainee proportion and expert administrations.

One pretty far of Norway's coast, there is an island in the Outer Oslofjord that is home to Bastøy Prison, which is known as the "world's first human ecological prison." This 80-building low-security jail complex houses only 115 hoodlums whose feelings incorporate the most savage and vile violations. Killers, attackers, and street pharmacists serve their time at Bastøy Prison. However the jail has no dividers, fences, or spiked metal. Bastøy Prison is an "open" jail design where there are no obstructions between the jail and the rest of the world, and a few detainees even drive to the terrain every day for their positions prior to getting back to the jail around evening time. About a third of Norwegian penitentiaries are open detainment facilities with Bastøy being the most well known. The objective of open penitentiaries is to help facilitate the progress among detainment and opportunity, and detainees at certain open jails will clean their own garments, own cell telephones, and approach the Internet. At Bastøy, the officers are not furnished, and coincide with the detainees. The officers and detainees together will in general livestock, cleave wood, play a game of cards, ski, play tennis, hold grills, cook, and take classes together. At 3:00 pm every day, most of the 69 officers and jail employees take a ship back to the terrain, leaving simply four officers to watch the jail overnight and on ends of the week. In reality, the island's detainees are liable for working the ship to and from Bastøy. The primary obligation of the prison guards is to tally the detainees: once toward the beginning of the day, twice during the day at their work environments, once before supper, and once around evening time.

It is nothing unexpected that Bastøy Prison has been depicted as perhaps the most liberal detainment facilities in the world. The jail has been run for a very long time at this point, and is by all accounts viable. The jail's recidivism rate is simply 16%, which is even lower than the Norwegian recidivism rate in general and far lower than the American recidivism rate. Without a doubt, Bastøy Prison's recidivism rate is the least rate for any jail in all of Europe despite holding brutal lawbreakers.

The detainees live in collective houses furnished with kitchens, parlors, and private rooms. The island furnishes detainees with an abundance of entertainment openings including skiing, fishing, running, strength preparing, horseback riding, and swimming at their own private sea shore. The detainees approach a cinema, tanning bed, and two ski bounces. A portion of the detainees formed the Bastøy Blues Band, and they were allowed consent to leave the island to go to a performance where they were an initial represent ZZ Top. The jail's structures incorporate a congregation, school, library, and supermarket. Inmates can spend their brought in cash at the grocery store on premium products, for example, cacao chocolate and aloe-vera juice. The island additionally includes a public sea shore open to all regular folks that the detainees are not permitted to get to. Be that as it may, no wall or blockades separate the public sea shore from the remainder of the island, and getting inquisitive travelers far from the detainees has demonstrated more troublesome than getting detainees far from the public sea shore.

Bastøy Prison is self-supportable and financially dependable. Detainees develop natural vegetables and raise chickens, cows, and sheep. The couple of vehicles situated on the island all sudden spike in demand for biodiesel. In any case, the favored method of transportation is strolling, bicycling or utilizing the island's six ponies, which the detainees approach ride. A large number of the prisoners own their own bikes, which can be fixed at the island's bike auto shop. The jail's offices are warmed by wood cleaved on the island by detainees, and the island's waste produces its capacity. Without a doubt, the detainees even approach cutting apparatuses that they use to chop down trees for kindling. This is all essential for Bastøy's model of recovery. By making the detainees liable for the livestock and the consistent running of the jail, the objective is to ingrain a feeling of obligation, duty, and morals in the detainees. In contrast to ordinary penitentiaries, there isn't tight command over the detainees' lives, and they should keep their own timetables. The detainees are liable for preparing their own dinners, arriving as expected for their jail occupations, and going to any necessary classes, which remember subjects for being against medication and hostile to savagery.

Detainees should apply to carry out their punishments at Bastøy. The verifying cycle decides if the detainees will probably undermine or disturb the framework set up. Yet, it is not necessarily the case that genuine, savage criminals don't serve their time here.Norway's most infamous chronic executioner, Arnfinn Nesset, spent time in jail at Bastøy Prison. Nesset was a medical caretaker and nursing home chief that was sentenced for killing 22 of his older patients by harming. He is thought to have slaughtered up to 138 of his patients dependent on numerous other people who passed on dubiously. Nesset was condemned to 21 years in jail, Norway's most extreme sentence, and preventive detainment. Notwithstanding, Nesset—and stress that he is the most scandalous chronic executioner in Norway's set of experiences—was delivered from jail following 12 years for good conduct at Bastøy Prison.

In spite of the moderately little management and complete absence of dividers or fencing, there has been only one departure endeavor in Bastøy Prison's 34-year history. Two prisoners attempted to return a boat to shore, yet inverted and were gotten. Without a doubt, Arne Nilsen,

Bastøy's chief tells detainees upon appearance, "in the event that you flee, kindly phone us at the earliest opportunity so we realize you are OK and won't have to utilize helicopters." At Bastøy, there are not really any recorded reports of viciousness, and there is for all intents and purposes no ill will between the watchmen and detainees. There is a solid impetus to act well at Bastøy Prison since spending time in jail there is an advantage that can be renounced. Despite the fact that all Norwegian jails are incredibly decent, Bastøy remains a cut above.Arne Nilsen, the head of Bastøy Prison, gets numerous postcards from delivered detainees who express gratitude toward him and Bastøy for improving their lives to such an extent.

The detainees at Bastøy are not permitted cell phones, yet the island has five telephone corners accessible for the prisoners. Detainees can make calls in the mornings and evenings. Moreover, detainees are permitted visits from pariahs three times each week, including biological urge satisfying arrangements.

One final benefit of Bastøy Prison is that it is far less expensive to run than common penitentiaries on the grounds that the jail utilizes far less officials, particularly overnight, and the island is to a great extent independent with the officers and detainees living off of the land and the their rewards for all the hard work. To be sure, the jail has a few farmhouses that produce eggs and other homestead products that are packaged and sold on the territory, turning out a revenue stream for the jail.

Norway's other most renowned jail is Halden Prison, which has an alternate model from Bastøy yet is in any case luxurious, costing230 million dollars to construct. After visiting, American jail superintendent James Conway depicted Halden as "jail ideal world," and closed, "I don't figure you can get any more liberal—other than giving the detainees the keys." Halden Prison opened in 2010, and is situated on a 75-section of land facility with the ability to hold 252 prisoners, making it Norway's second biggest jail. 12 sections of land of the office comprise of blueberry backwoods. With regards to the framework's objectives, Halden is intended to look after regularity, so there are no bars on the windows, and the officers and inmates maintain companionships. The whole jail was intended to imitate a little town to remind detainees that they are as yet a piece of society. Halden Prison's chief, Are Hoidel, expressed, "detainees in Norwegian jail are returning to the general public. Do you need individuals who are furious or individuals who are rehabilitated?"

To date, no prisoner has ever endeavored to escape from Halden Prison.

Halden Prison rehabilitates and reintegrates its detainees through various professional projects including gathering workshops, carpentry, and a chronicle studio. The officials coordinate exercises for the detainees from 8:00 toward the beginning of the day until 8:00 at night to guarantee that they stay productive and locked in. The prisoners do not wear uniforms and effectively mix in with the restorative officers.The officials—half of whom are female—don't convey weapons, and they play sports and eat suppers with the detainees.

Be that as it may, Halden Prison more intently takes after a customary jail than Bastøy. The jail is separated into building units, which each house 84 detainees. The individual cells are roomy, and each ten prisoners share a typical room. Singular cells have their own little fridges, televisions, and bathrooms with clay tiling while the basic territories have Xboxes, dartboards, and a completely prepared kitchen. What's more, truly, the kitchen contains sharp forks and blades that the detainees have full, solo admittance to. Like at Bastøy, the detainees have open admittance to a wide scope of apparatuses such as hammers and saws that they may require for their jail jobs. The jail likewise has a detached structure where wrongdoers can have their families for overnight stays. Prisoners even have admittance to the Internet, in spite of the fact that entrance is directed and certain sites are confined.

Maybe Halden's most fascinating element is its elite account studio that the detainees and officials the same appreciate. After survey the studio, American jail superintendent

James Conway announced, "I'm struggling accepting that I'm in a jail." Music exercises are offered so the prisoners can figure out how to play instruments, sing, and handle the sound hardware. For sure, three of Halden's detainees showed up on Idol, Norway's form of American Idol. Halden Prison is really during the time spent creating its first melodic; normally the detainees will be the stars.

Halden Prison has an amazing indoor rec center total with a stone climbing divider. The jail keeps a little emergency clinic and cutting edge dental specialist's office to guarantee that the detainees have quality admittance to their ensured wellbeing and dental consideration. Also, the jail's extensive grounds give open air fields to play sports like soccer and b-ball. Running path befuddle the extensive woodlands. The grounds are packed with nature, as the jail was intended to have numerous enormous trees. The trees effectively obscure the divider around the jail, which keeps up the feeling of routineness for the detainees. An extra 1,000,000 dollars was spent on artworks, photos, and light installations to make a warm, cozy environment for the jail. Indeed, even the jail's outside divider is decorated with fine art. Incredible idea went into the shades of the jail's numerous structures: the outside dividers are earthy colored to mix in with nature, the cell dividers are green to make an alleviating air, the working regions are splendid orange to inspire energy, and the guesthouse's intimate room is a blazing red. Overall, the inside decorator used 18 distinct tones all through the jail.

Halden Prison a hefty accentuation on schooling and occupation preparing. Detainees have a scope of alternatives for occupations, and get

60 Norwegian Krone—$7.75 in American money—every day's worth of effort. The jail clinician broadcasts that inmates should take their minds off jail and spotlight on planning for life in the outside world. Prisoners appear to be taking his guidance, as they train to become carpenters, repairmen, and more. The "kitchen lab" shows detainees the essentials of nourishment and cooking, with the goal that they can get ready solid dinners for themselves and train for professions as food providers, gourmet specialists, and waiters.

In Norway, rehabilitation through formal education has been a long – term priority in the criminal service. Education is considered as one of the most significant tool to master life after ending sentencing and works as a great crime prevention tool. Further, education in jail intends to expand the detainee's ability. Education can build work possibilities and subsequently, a way to go by to meet day to day requirements upon release, which will prevent recidivism. Education will assist detainees to exploit their capacities and understand their objectives in life. Education is key to reducing recidivism and the Norwegian government understood it in 2008 when it first implemented education for its inmates and the results have been there for all to see.

To prepare a person to not commit crime again should be the idea of a prison and the idea of prison shouldn't be to haunt the citizen from the place in order to maintain law and order in society. A lot many countries, including India practice this method of scaring the population from going to jail rather than working on things that cause crime in the first place. If there's a robber, make him employable, if there's a physical abuser, take him to a psychologist, if the causes of crimes are cured which happens to be the responsibility of the State then there shall be no crime and this is what Norway precisely works upon, it works on creating a better environment for its inmates for when they are released. The State as known is not successful in curing these social causes, especially in India, hence they adopt a simpler method, to instill fear of going through immense pain and humiliation in the population if one commits a crime. But fear shall last only so long whereas education stays forever.

At last, we should also remember that Norway is a small country compared to India in size and in population, it is a homogenous society whereas India is considerably the most heterogeneous society on the face of earth and statistically a very rich community than India when we compare the per capita income of both countries and hence it is easier to say such a model cannot exist in a large country like India but what's the harm in trying one proven working system?

Chapter 5: Prisoner's Human Rights

Ever since the Universal Declaration of Human Rights was passed in the General Assembly of the United Nations, the organization has always considered Human Rights of citizens across the world of paramount importance. It has created a special wing for looking into Human Rights violations by the name of Human Rights Council and it holds a very high importance in the Organization. As recent as in early 2021, the body commented upon the Farmers protest against certain agricultural laws wherein the Government decided to shut-down internet services and since it is a body of the United Nations, anything coming out of that office is alarming for any country as it has the ability to affect the international reputation of that country. Adhering to the principles of the Human Rights Council is always considered ideal.

The idea of human rights has a long history and the prison is considered as a place in which individuals are physically confined and are deprived of personal freedom to a certain extent. Prison holds a very important position in the criminal justice system, especially one like India wherein majority of the prison population is under-trial because one can be arrested on account of almost any and every offence that one can think of. There might be prisons which are meant exclusively for adults, children, females, convicted prisoners, under-trials etc and the objective of such imprisonment of these class of prisoners may vary from country to country. Some may intend it to be punitive, some may intend to create deterrence in their society, others may intend it to be either reformative or rehabilitative for the inmates, it could be any of these but the primary purpose of imprisonment is to protect society against criminals in our legal system. For this the state applies punitive measures but it is vile because the recidivism rate has forced the policy-makers and law-makers to come up with something new that would work in the current social system. Not to forget, the United Nations guidelines for the treatment of prisoners is also to be followed along with the various human rights legislations as well as judicial decisions have paved a way for the government to make more humanitarian laws for the prisoners. The state is under legal obligation for protecting its subjects and for the compliance of which citizens are given certain basic privileges recognized by the Constitution of India and other legislations. However, the enhancement of rights of the prisoners raises a question as to what extent it is viable under Article 21 to incorporate within its ambit. These are questions raised considering what about the rights of the victims of their offences and to what extent the arena of rights of the prisoners can be enhanced under the umbrella of human rights so as to not violate the human rights of the victims who have suffered the consequences of the offence committed upon them.

The main human rights issue of under trials is delay in trial of cases. Right to speedy trial is a right to life and personal liberty of a prisoner that has been guaranteed under Article 21 of the Constitution through its reading in various decisions pronounced by the Apex Court which ensures just, fair and reasonable procedure. However, in many prisons up to eighty percent prisoners in the country are undertrials, and in some cases they are not released even after being granted the bail because they aren't able to furnish surety bonds due to lack of money or verification of address, or availability of a guarantor on the conditions set by law, as they don't have that kind of resources at their disposal. The speedy trial of offenders is one of the basic objectives of the criminal justice delivery system. Once the cognizance of the accusation is taken by the court then the trial has to be conducted expeditiously so as to punish the guilty and to absolve the innocent. Everyone is said to be presumed innocent until proven guilty yet there exists no disparity in treating the two in most cases. So, the quality or innocence of the accused has to be determined as quickly as possible.

In reference to the Constitution of India and human rights references are available since 1985. The Constitution of India Bill, 1985, popularly known as Home Rule Bill, the M. Chelmsford report, 1918, talks about certain fundamental rights. The Commonwealth of India Bill, 1925 and the Moti Lal Nehru Committee Report,1928 also indicate about the efforts for human rights in India, but the real process started with the adoption of the famous Karachi resolution of 1931.[167] On December 13, 1946 the objective's resolution moved by Pt. Jawaharlal Nehru and the same was unanimously adopted by the Constituent Assembly on January 22, 1947. The principles were laid down in fundamental documents were duly considered and applied by the framers of the Constitution while drawing up the Indian Constitution. The preamble of the Indian Constitution has all the rights as guarantees and grants freedoms contemplated in the same document. Human Rights of the prisoners in India can be seen by two different perspectives which are Constitutional status and development of human rights and

---

[167] Khwaja Abdul Muntaqim, *Protection of Human Rights: National & International Perspectives*, 27. Law Publishers (India) Pvt. Ltd.

prison reforms to implement the constitutional human rights of prisoners.

In reference with Human Rights there is a common rule and well accepted universally that all human beings have the right to basic human rights without any discrimination. Prisoners are also not the exception to this principle. Since, the Indian social system is supposedly based on non – violence, respect and legal system is based on the rule of natural justice, including rule of law, therefore, prisoner's rights are subject matters of human rights and almost all basic human rights are conferred upon the individuals by the Constitution. Although there are no specific rights to the prisoners mentioned in the Constitution, the prisoners remain a person as per constitutional view, thereby the basic human rights of prisoners are protected by the Constitution itself. It has also made clear from the Indian judicial system that human beings are born equal in dignity and rights, so there can be no discrimination on the basis of any ground, though some restrictions may be imposed in some specific cases. It is the human life that requires human rights. These rights are moral claims and are inalienable and is inherent in all individuals, irrespective of their caste, colour, creed, and place of birth, sex, or any other consideration. These claims are articulated and formulated in what is in present day known as Human Rights. The definition of the word prisoner is also not mentioned in about any kind of negative impact or in violation of human rights. Being in a civilized society which is governed by law and a system as such, it is essential to ensure the dignity of every citizen, even if the person is confined or imprisoned because of his wrong, he is entitled to his rights that should be unaffected by the punishment for wrongs, simply because if a person under – trial, his rights cannot be discarded as a whole.

UDHR, 1948 also talks about that motto if its which is "No one shall be subject to torture or cruel, inhuman or degrading treatment or punishment".

The Constitution of India has a vital role in formulating the basic human rights of the people and the Prisoners also have the basic human rights protected by the same which can not be taken away from them. The Indian Constitution clearly mentions the fundamental rights and duties to all its citizens but does not explicitly mentions any list of rights for prisoners nor does it give any curtailment in the list of fundamental rights. The fundamental rights guaranteed by the Constitution is not absolute in nature as the state always has power to impose certain restrictions on it as it deems proper. The status of a convicted person or that of an incarcerated person is different from a common citizen, as he is to undergo prison sentence of a defined period and prisons are considered as a closed institution due to which such person cannot claim all the fundamental rights available to a common citizen and the prison administration has been granted to make certain rules as provided in the prison manuals for the operating of the prisons through imposing certain restrictions upon the prisoners for what is considered to maintain order. But it never means that the prison administration has powers to curtail prisoner's basic and fundamental human rights like right to life, medical assistance and equality etc. The Judiciary while considering various cases clearly interpreted the carious Articles and its implied meaning and conferred more rights to the people.

The Article 14 of the Constitution of India, gives the right to equality and equal protection before the laws. So, prisoners have their own rights grantcd by thc Constitution. If anything contrary to it is committed on a prisoner, by the police, it is considered as a violation of rights and it requires to be brought to the attention of the Judiciary and the Legislature. The right to meet visitors and lawyers are embedded through Article 14 and Article 21 and such rights are reasonable and non – arbitrary. Even prison regulations recognize the rights of prisoners to have interviews with a legal advisor necessary, in a reasonable manner. The right to free legal aid is also provided under Article 14 and 21. In Maneka Gandhi vs. Union of India (AIR 1978 SC 597), the Supreme Court held that the personal liberty of an individual can be restrained only in accordance with law and by the procedure established in law and such procedure must be just, fair and reasonable. In the case of Maneka Gandhi, the Attorney General stated that the Government has agreed to consider the representation of the petitioner. The Apex Court held that since the defect of the order was removed, the right to travel of the petitioner was deprived only in accordance with the proecedure established by law in Passport Act and hence the order was found to not be a violation of Article 14, 19(1) (a), or 21 of the Indian Constitution. Again in Madhukar Bhagwan Jambhale vs. State of Maharashtra (1984 [2] Bom. Cr. Cases 709) it has been decided by the court that Rule 17 (ix) of the Maharashtra Prison (Facilitates to Prisoners) Rules, 1962, is discriminatory and violative of Article 14 of the Constitution and must therefore, be struck down. A prisoner is entitled to send welfare letters to prisoners in the prisons, whether such prisoners are relatives or not.

Article 15 of the Indian Constitution deals with the Prohibition of discrimination on the grounds of religion, race, caste, sex or place of birth. This Article says that the State shall not discriminate any person on the basis of his or her religion, race, sex, and place of birth or any of them. Under article 15 (3) & (4), the Government can make special provisions for women & children and for a group of citizens who are economically and socially backward. It is the rights of a prisoner to live inside the prison without discrimination. The Constitution of India guarantees Right against Discrimination to each person. Here the person also includes prisoners, so a prisoner has complete rights against discrimination on the ground of religion, race, caste, sex or place of birth.

Article 19 of the Constitution deals with the Rights to Freedom which includes six freedoms and all these are under reasonable restriction under various sub-clauses of the same Article. Among these freedoms right to freedom of speech and expression and freedom to become a member of an association are available to prisoners, but all other freedoms like right to movement, right to reside and settlement anywhere in India, right to profession occupation, trade or business cannot available to the prisoners. To handcuff is to hoop harshly and to punish humiliatingly. The minimum freedom of movement, under which a detainee is entitled to under Article 19, cannot be cut down by the application of handcuffs. Handcuffs must be the last refuge as there are other ways for ensuring security. Article 20(1) of the Constitution, protect the person from ex post facto laws or retroactive criminal legislation; Article 20(2), provides that no person shall be put into trouble twice, for the same offenses, (rights against double jeopardy) and Article 20(3), provides for the protection against „testimonial compulsion. On the question of human rights in criminal administration in reference to handcuffs and fetters it can be considered that Articles 20, 21 and 22 of the Constitution are relevant to the administration of criminal justice[168]. Right to life under Article 21 is also one of the important rights given by the constitution and guarantees the right of personal liberty and thereby prohibits any inhuman, cruel or degrading treatment to any person whether he is a national or a foreigner. Article 21 Protection of life

---

[168] K. Sarkar, *Public Interest Litigations and Public Nuisances (Second Edition)*, 761, Orient Publishing Company: Prayagraj, 2009

and personal liberty as "No person shall be deprived of his or personal liberty except according to procedure established by law". Here in context to deprivation Prison is treated as any place which has been declared by the Government, by general or special order, to be a subsidiary jail, or any reformative, brutal institution or other institution of a like nature. And Confinement in a prison refers to confinement in a prison, by whatever form of words, include references to confinement or detention in a prison under any law providing for prevention detention. Thus the above mentioned provisions have not any type of violation of human rights of prisoners, further life under Article 21 has extended meaning given to life to the word and those citizens who are detained in prison either as under-trails or as convicts, all are entitled to the benefit of the guarantees subject to reasonable restriction[169]. In

Maneka Gandhi v. Union of India the Supreme Court has widened the concept life under Article 21 and conferred more rights to lead dignified life e.g., the rights of speedy trail, right to practice religion and right to communication etc. but all thcsc rights are subjected to restriction as prescribed under prison manual and Constitution. Right to speedy trial is a fundamental right of a prisoner implicit in Article 21 of the Constitution. It ensures just, fair and reasonable procedure[170]. In Prem Shankar v. Delhi Administration[171] the Supreme Court held that Handcuffing should be resorted to only when there is clear and present danger of escape from the police control. Handcuffing is held to be prima facie in human and therefore unreasonable and thus is in violation of Article 21. In Francis Coralie

---

169 Sheela Barse vs. State of Maharashtra, 1988 (1) Bom. Cr. Cases 58 at 64
170 Hussainara Khatoon (II) vs. Home Secretary, State of Bihar, (1980) 1 SCC 81.
171 AIR 1980 SC 1579

Mullin v. The Administrator, Union Territory of Delhi[172] the Supreme Court held that the Right to Life protected under Article 21 is not confined merely to the right of physical existence but it also includes within its broad matrix the right to the use of every faculty or limb through which life is enjoyed as also the right to live with basic human dignity. In Sunil Batra (II)[173], arising out of a letter written by Sunil Batra to one of the judges of the Supreme Court alleging that a warden in Tihar Jail had caused bleeding injury to a convict by name Prem Chand by forcing a stick into his anus, the Court liberalized the procedural rigidities of tine writ of habeas corpus and employed the writ, following the American cases for the oversight of state penal machinery and for the condemnation of the brutalities and tortures inflicted on the prisoners. On

---

[172] AIR 1980 SC 1585
[173] AIR 1981 SC 745

the basis of this, the Supreme Court treated Batra's letter as a petition for habeas corpus and issued the writ to the Lieutenant Governor of Delhi and the Superintendent of Central Jail ordering that Prem Chand should not be subjected to torture and the wound on his person should receive proper medical attention[174]. In Citizen for Democracy v. State of Assam[175] the Court treated the letter as a petition under Article 32 and held that handcuffing and in addition, tying with ropes of the patient prisoners who are admitted in the hospitals, are violations of human rights guaranteed under Article 21 of the Constitution.

In Hoskot[176], the Court held "If a prisoner sentenced to imprisonment, is virtually unable to exercise his constitutional and statutory right of appeal, inclusive of special leave

---

[174] M. C. Valsan. *Rights of Prisoners: An Evolving Jurisprudence*, 2013, 58. (Unpublished Ph.D. Dissertation, Cochin University of Science and Technologies.
[175] AIR 1995 SCC 743
[176] AIR 1975 SC 1548

appeal, for want of legal assistance, there is implicit in the court under Article 142 read with Articles 21 and 39A of the Constitution, power to assign counsel for such imprisoned individual for doing complete justice. This is a necessary incident of the right of appeal conferred by the Code and allowed by Article 136 of the Constitution. The inference is inevitable that this is a State's duty and not Government's charity". After a period of six year the Supreme Court again said in Khatri v. State of Bihar[177] that the right to free legal services is clearly an essential ingredient of reasonable, fair and just procedure a person accused of an offence and it is implicit in the guarantee of Article 21.

The history of the modern Indian prison system started from the beginning of the British colonial era in India. When the British conquered

---

[177] AIR 1981 SC 928

India, there was no uniformity in civil and criminal procedural system. The system of punishments differs from region to region and ruler to ruler. When the British conquered different princely states, each state followed different punishment system. This was one of the issues faced by the British. In order to overcome the issue, the then British government appointed a committee, namely Prison Discipline Committee under the Chairmanship of T B Macaulay in 1835. The Committee submitted the report in 1838 and recommended increased rigorousness of treatment while rejecting all humanitarian needs and reforms for the prisoners. Following the recommendation new central prisons were constructed and wrong doers placed behind the bars.

Reformation through incarceration was the main objectives of the construction of new jails. As per the recommendation of T. B.Macaulay

Committee the Government constructed the prisons and deprived various draconian punishment methods such as mutilation, branding etc. as a part of implementation of reformative methods they constructed Schools, Hospitals and Factories etc. The prison administration also established industries inside the prisons and assigned various kinds of works to the prisoners with remunerations.

Although the reformation was the main objectives of the prison administration in the British India, human rights violations was common in every prison. Prisoners were subjected to severe tortures, even juvenile offenders were subjected to flogging and the prison administration discriminated the prisoners on the basis of caste, religion and race. The prison administration did not provided proper space to follow religious belief. In the name of discipline, the prison administration denied to religious rights and often confiscates their religious properties. In addition to this, the prison administration tortured the prisoners to provide harder works without providing proper remuneration.

India became a Republic on 26th January, 1950, and the Constitution of India, with a new spirit, was promulgated; but unfortunately, most of the pre-independence laws (the Indian Penal Code, 1860. The Prison Act, 1894, the Prisoners Act, 1900, the Identification of Prisoners Act, 1920 and the Punjab Jail Manual, 1898) though at variance with the spirit of the Constitution of India, continued in operation. In 1952, Walter C. Reciles an American Expert on prison administration, was invited from UNO and a draft on Modal Prison Laws and manuals were prepared in 1954, but these could not become the part of law. A. N. Mulla Report, 1980-1983, were also appointed for the purpose of amending the prison laws. After that the government of India, under the severe criticism of violation of Human Rights, has appointed a National Human Rights Commission and this has started an investigation for revamping the prison administration for systematic reforms. But in actual the reports of the above committees or commission could not get the approval of the legislature and could not become the part of the law of the land. And finally the Judiciary has interfered in the matter and treated a letter as a writ petition and by an elaborate judgment allowed the petition and issued directions inclusive of one for taking suitable action against the erring official to the Ministry of Home Affairs and all State Governments[178].

Though the Constitution of India has a wide category of human rights for all, the prisoners are also protected under this category. At the time of implementation of Constitution of India, Constitutional Makers have taken appropriate steps by inserting chapter of fundamental rights. The Judiciary has also contributed more by developing the dimensions of fundamental rights and also tried to resolve the various issues being faced by the prisoners. The Supreme Court and High Courts while considering various cases clearly interpreted the various Articles and its implied meaning and conferred more rights to the prisoners. While considering petitions regarding the issues of prisoners the Supreme Court laid down various guidelines to be followed by the prison administration, police and other investigative agencies. Even the Court has

---

[178] Sunil Batra vs. Delhi Administration, AIR 1980 SC 1579

considered the report of newspaper and letter sent by the prisoners in regard to the pathetic situations of prisoners as Writ petition and directed to the government to take proper actions to resolve the issues. If a prisoner sentenced to imprisonment, is virtually unable to exercise his constitutional and statutory right of appeal, for want of legal assistance, there is implicit in the court under article 142 read with article 21 and 39 A of the Constitution, power to assign council for such imprisoned individual for doing complete justice. Where the prisoner is disabled from engaging a lawyer, on reasonable grounds such as indigence or incommunicado situation, the court shall, if the circumstances of the case, the gravity of the sentence, and the ends of justice so required, assign competent counsel for the prisoners defense, provided the party doesn't object to that lawyer. Role of the policy and lawmakers have also been remained considerable on the aspect of prisoner human rights. Various commission and committees have done redressal works for prisoners and also works for introducing the reformative measures by recommending an e-governance system a step towards Jail reforms for ensuring the protection of human rights to the prisoners.

Chapter 6: You Hate Overcrowded Metro, they live in Overcrowded Halls!

Nobody likes empty spaces, an empty mall or an empty market street or an empty metro train can be a bit scary but at the same time these very things when overcrowded can make the experience horrible too. We need to strike the right balance when it comes to having people at public spaces. India naturally is a densely populated country and to ask for a thing to not be overcrowded is a huge ask but yet a very legitimate one.

At the point when the prison population exceeds its approved limit of convenience, it is then referred to as Overcrowding. Overcrowding in the prisons is a violation of human rights of the prisoners as it brings down the general living standards of the prisoners. It similarly causes deterrence in the reorganization process. The opinion of Prison

Administrators on this is that it's hard to start and proceed with remedial measures. The overall prison population according to the International Center for Prison Studies, Kings College, London (2006) stood at 9.45 million as against the total world population of 6.65 Billion. This adds up to 0.14 percent of the aggregate population being held up in prisons. Congestion is pervasive in relatively every nation in one frame or the other. Other than creating and immature nations of Africa and Asia, created nations like United States of America, Japan and United Kingdom are likewise confronting this problem.' One of America's most concerning issues today is the congestion of penitentiaries. This started when the number of inhabitants in prisoners began to take off in the 1980's. With the expansion of attackers, killers, and medication merchants soaring, there are clear motivations to this overpopulation in jail seen today.

The modern prison in India originated with the Minute by T. B. Macaulay in 1835. A committee namely Prison Discipline Committee, was appointed, which submitted its report on 1838. The contemporary Prison organization in India is therefore an inheritance of British run the show. It depends on the idea that the best criminal code can be of little use to a group unless there is great apparatus for the curse of disciplines. In 1864, the Second Commission of Inquiry into Jail Management and Discipline made comparable suggestions as the 1836 Committee. Likewise, this Commission made some particular proposals with respect to convenience for detainees, change in eat less carbs, apparel, bedding and restorative care. In 1877, a Conference of Experts met to ask into jail organization. The meeting proposed the order of a jail law and a draft charge was readied. In 1888, the Fourth Jail Commission was designated. Based on its proposal, a united jail charge was defined.

It is the Prisons Act, 1894, based on which the present correctional facility administration and organization works in India. This Act has barely experienced any generous change. In any case, the procedure of survey of the jail issues in India proceeded even after this. In the report of the Indian Jail Committee 1919-20, without precedent for the historical backdrop of penitentiaries, 'reconstruction and recovery' of guilty parties were recognized as the targets of the jail administrator. The Government of India Act, 1935, brought about the exchange of the subject of prisons from the middle rundown to the control of commonplace governments and subsequently additionally decreased the likelihood of uniform usage of a jail approach at the national level.

In 1960, the Committee put together the Model Prison Manual (MPM) and presented it to the Government of India for use. The MPM 1960 is the guiding principle upon which the current Indian jail administration is based. The Ministry of Home Affairs, Government of India, formed a working group on detention facilities in 1972, based on the Model Prison Manual. In its study, it stressed the importance of a national approach to prisons. It also made a crucial proposal about the order and treatment of guilty parties, as well as establishing criteria.

In 1980, the Indian government formed a Committee on Jail Reform, which was chaired by Justice A. N. Mulla. The Committee's main aim was to examine the rules, guidelines, and controls with the overall goal of protecting society and rehabilitating wrongdoers in mind. In 1983, the Mulla Committee issued its report.

The Justice Krishna Iyer Committee was appointed by the Indian government in 1987 to investigate the situation of female detainees in the country. It has been proposed that more women be enlisted in the police force because of their unique role in dealing with female and youngster criminals.

In several parts of India, prisons are overcrowded. In 1995, for example, there were 8500 prisoners in Delhi's Tihar Jail, compared to a total of 2500. Congestion has the negative effect of preventing segregation among convicts, both those who have been rebuffed for serious crimes and those who have been rebuffed for minor offences. As a result, solidified prisoners can have a broader effect on various detainees. Since there aren't enough elective places where they can be bound, juvenile criminals are forced to interact with solidified hoodlums and are more likely to become proficient wrongdoers. It is in this setting the issue of congestion in detainment facilities should be handled in right sincere.

The lack of military quarters and cells is a major factor in jail overcrowding. India's population is steadily increasing, which has coincided with an increase in criminal activity; the number of prisoners is also rapidly increasing. In 2006, India's detention facilities had the capacity to accommodate 2,63,911 inmates. However, the total number of people in jail in that year was 3,73,271. A shortfall of 1,09,360 was noted along these lines. From the monetary year 2002-2003, the trend in Indian jails shows an increase in congestion in spite of the expansion of crisp limit under the Modernization of Prison Scheme promoted by the Ministry of

Home Affairs, India, in collaboration with the States.

While an increase in the number of inmates is likely to reduce misconduct, increasing wrongdoing rates also result in larger prison populations. To break the stalemate, this paper uses the status of a state's prison stuffing case as a tool for tracking changes in the jail population. Congestion has been shown to have a negative effect on jail populations, but it is unlikely to be linked to fluctuations in the wrongdoing rate other than by its impact on jail populations. Incrementing results in assessments of the scope of abuse as well as the number of prisoners that are many times more significant than previous assessments. The bulk of the corruption classes investigated yielded positive results.

Disposal of programmes, budget cuts, and organisational improvements in social services. Individuals who lack access to assets turn to the underground economy to feed themselves and their families, resulting in detainees. The following are some examples:

- The General Relief Program in Massachusetts, a 200-year-old welfare programme for needy single citizens, will be phased out.

- Welfare rolls are being cut in the Assistance to Families with Dependent Children (AFDC) programme.

The term "War on Drugs" is usually associated with the United States government's fight against illegal drugs. In 1969, US President Richard Nixon coined the word. A few medication plans, military guidance and assistance, and assistance from taking an interest nations are all part of the War on Drugs. The US government hopes to demoralise and eliminate the production, circulation, and use of illegal drugs through this battle. The increase in the number of prisoners is expected as a result of the war on illegal drugs. In 1980, 15 drug-related prisoners were discovered in a crowd of 100,000 people. By 1996, the number of prescription convicts had increased to 148 per 100,000 people. The overall number of prisoners was influenced by the rate of growth in the number of medication convicts.

To put it bluntly, most detainees' proficiency levels are appalling, falling well short of what is generally expected by companies for even the most inept jobs. As a result, it should come as no surprise that detainees who enrol in instruction and preparation services have a higher work rate and a lower recidivism rate than those who do not. That isn't to say that education is a panacea for the country's wrongdoing problem and the resulting prison overcrowding. In any case, it's a solid sign that instruction is a critical factor not just in shielding individuals from going to jail in any case yet in addition in keeping them out once they have been discharged.

Another major aspect of the problem is the socioeconomic and financial inequality, which contributes to prisoners having less access to high-quality educational opportunities prior to their incarceration. Living in a low-income area often means having access to low-quality tutoring. According to the United States Department of Education, more than 40% of low-wage schools do not receive adequate state and national educational funding, meaning that they have less money to spend on supplies, foundation, and teachers. Furthermore, since young understudies in low-wage families will feel compelled to contribute financially to their struggling family, they will most likely drop out to do so. The insufficient jail base has an immediate and detrimental impact on the framework, resulting in overcrowding. Since it is a fact that is available all over the locale, old institutions that were often not prepared for detention facilities need space and the least states with better than average service, according to global experts. Overpopulation other than being a genuine Bad in itself, influences the states of cleanliness, wellbeing, sustenance, rest and security. Leased space of square metres for their private life, strolling and physical exercises, giving an amount of drinking water for individual cleanliness, clothing and hydration and Pavilions must have proper light, ventilation and natural air.

In India, detention facilities have an endorsed standard of 49030 jail personnel at various positions, with the current staff quality being about 40000.The ratio of jail personnel to inmates is approximately 1:7. It means that only one jail officer is available for every seven detainees, while in the UK, two jail officers are available for every three detainees.

In India, legal counsel for those who cannot bear to retain counsel is only available during the trial, not when the prisoner is taken to the remand court. Although the vast majority of prisoners, both that in solitary confinement and those in prison, have not been tried, the absence of a legal representative before the point of trial significantly lowers the assessment of the country's legal representation arrangement for vulnerable citizens. Legal counsel is not readily available at a time when a large number of people need it.

In 1998, in Bhopal, a workshop organized by Commonwealth Human

Rights Watch focused on a few issues related to lawful guide. It was pointed out that 70% of the inmates are uneducated and have no understanding of their rights.

Blackmail by jail workers, and its less violent conclusion, protect defilement, is common in detention centres around the world. These concerns are unsurprising given the significant influence that watchmen wielded over prisoners, but the low pay rates that gatekeepers are generally paid irritate them greatly. Detainees augment gatekeepers' pay rates with fixes in exchange for stash or special care. Capable prisoners in a few offices in Colombia, India, and Mexico luxuriated in PDAs, nutritious diets, and comfortable lodgings, while their less fortunate brethren suffered from a lack of sanitation.

Overcrowding in jails and exorbitant jail rates are a problem in, for all intents and purposes, every state in the United States. One unique viewpoint is that we do not have penitentiaries in a cutting-edge, diverse world. This is a concept that I strongly condemn. The first and most obvious argument about jail is that we need detention facilities; there are some particularly bad people for whom therapy will be ineffective, and allowing them to live in the open would result in devastation with the hope of complimentary natives.

Another fascinating perspective is that the more stringent we become in our criminal justice endorsements, the lower the likelihood of corruption.

I can't help but disagree with this viewpoint. Professional criminals do not think in the same way as well-behaved locals do. For others, going to prison is an unavoidable consequence of crime. For some, being able to enter prison is a luxury. It makes no difference how strong the endorsement is if a suspect believes he or she will not be apprehended. The conviction of discipline is more important than its severity or even its pace.

The main drivers of high rates of detention and jail congestion must be reasonably addressed, assuming that they have been precisely and thoroughly investigated and understood, and if open strategies concerning wrongdoing and criminal equity are truly far-reaching, addressing every significant angle, rather than just the "criminal equity" related variables of the issue. Breaking down the specific causes of congestion in any given situation and addressing the root causes of wrongdoing and detention is critical to the long-term success of techniques that aim to reduce congestion and detention rates. This factor was discussed at the Workshop on Strategies to Reduce Overcrowding in Correctional Facilities, held in April

2010 in Salvador, Brazil, as part of the Twelfth United Nations Congress on Crime Prevention and Criminal Justice.

Except under the existing statute, judges are not required to impose minimum sentences on defendants. Only if the defendant has been convicted of a minor drug offence and has a relatively clear criminal record will a judge deviate from this protocol. That "escape valve" only extends to drug offenders; it does not apply to people facing mandatory minimum penalties for crimes that have little to do with drugs, such as white-collar crimes. As a result, a new "escape valve" may be made available to those facing a mandatory minimum sentence.

General evaluation plays a significant role in how governments decide about the best course of action in the face of misconduct. To legitimise correctional criminal equity systems, government officials often allude to the need to respond to open interest in tougher penalties. However, society as a whole is not a homogeneous entity with a single, static viewpoint. It is made up of a number of different and changing evaluations. Although many people believe that the courts are too sensitive, they also believe that prison is expensive and harmful, according to various reporters. Individuals tend to assist elective, non-correctional reactions when given the open door in reviews, particularly when questions provide sufficient insight into individual cases rather than being of a general nature.

Government detainees who complete the framework's primary tranquilization programme should have their sentences reduced by a year. In any case, due to overcrowding, the queue to get into the programme is so long that many of the guilty parties are just halfway through their sentences when they graduate. Expand the initiative such that any graduate receives a one-year reduction in their sentence.

Criminal justice reform policies must respond to the substances and circumstances in the general population in which they are to be implemented, while drawing on global expertise and great practise cases from various countries. Approaches should be based on a thorough analysis of the exact causes of congestion in the particular ward. The underlying far-reaching appraisal should include an assessment of the criminal equity system, including the profile of prisoners and trends in pre-trial detention and sentencing from an objective and realistic standpoint. Criminal equity changes can include administrative changes, amendments to condemning strategies, changes to functional and authoritative coordination and emotionally supportive networks, interest in the limit working of criminal equity performing artists, in instruction, and professional preparation, depending on the reasons for congestion and evaluated needs in prisons to enhance prisoners social reintegration prospects.

The involvement of political will is essential for success in reducing detention facility congestion. It is extremely difficult, if not impossible, to achieve genuine change without the will and strength to present arrangements and programmes that might challenge reformatory methodologies or require significant investment at first, as well as the will to sustain those policies for a long enough time to provide a solid reason for a long-term reduction in jail overcrowding.

With today's GPS advancements, checking innovations, and various forms of follow-up people, jail does not have to be the primary choice for relocating wrongdoers. A few people may be sentenced to house arrest, especially for peaceful wrongdoing. This could allow them to keep their job, telecommute, and still be monitored to ensure that their sentence is completed properly. If the ideas are given a chance, the solutions to prison congestion may be as simple as they sound. Texas has formally shown that new ideas in the criminal justice system can be implemented with ease.

A jail construction programme allows jail frameworks the opportunity to house convicted parties in safe and altruistic environments, which is an important aspect of any strategy to reduce jail overcrowding. In several countries, these proposals are either non-existent or have been obliterated due to budgetary constraints or higher-than-expected needs. Since the mid-1990s, the state of Texas in the United States has tripled the capacity of its detention facilities; however, it is expected that the state's current prison capacity will be exceeded by nearly 11,000 beds by 2010.

Detention has the potential to intensify rather than debilitate a child's misbehaviour. The United Nations has stated that children under the age of 12 should not be prosecuted. For those under the age of 18, traditional criminal justice goals, such as restraint and retribution, must be supplemented with educational and therapeutic interventions. Custodial remand and sentences can only be used as a last resort, for the shortest period of time, and in extreme circumstances. For children serving such sentences, small, accessible facilities with minimal security measures should be built.

The COVID-19 outbreak has also shown the mirror to the system that how vulnerable are we when we don't have adequate facilities to facilitate and no matter what, there was not enough time or resources to prepare for social distancing despite numerous courts only taking up Bail matters for hearing so that if there is a possibility of someone to be released from prison it should immediately be done so because inside the prison one is most vulnerable to the deadly disease and yet not all matters were heard upon because the number of bail applications is in such a huge number and almost all agencies functioning in criminal justice system is so understaffed that it was impossible for all to be heard. Supreme Court passed an order in a suo moto cognizance of the issue of risk of prisoners being infected and on 23rd March 2020 it passed an order in the same reiterating its order passed in Arnesh Kumar vs. State of Bihar[179] to avoid making arrests in case of persons charged with offences where maximum sentence was less than 7 years, as far as possible.

The Supreme Court issued a landmark decision in the case of Hussainara Khatoon vs. State of Bihar[180] regarding free legal aid. In addition, the Court held that a practise that holds such a large number of people behind bars without trial for such a long time cannot possibly be considered rational, just, or equitable in order to be in compliance with Article 21.

Despite the fact that a substantive re-examination would fail to interpret the complete panoply of Part-HI enjoyed by free natives, the Hon'ble Supreme Court held that detention does not spell the end of key rights. Article 21, when read in conjunction with Articles 19 (1) (d) and (5), is

[179] (2014) 8 SCC 273
[180] AIR 1979 SC 1369

suitable for a broader application than the glorious fiendishness that gave it birth, and should derive its meaning from the evolving models of goodness and poise that mark the progress of the developed society. The spirit of Article 21 is rational methodology. Article 19 (5) embodies the quintessence of restriction sensitivity, while Article 14 despises simple circumspection that devolves into self-aggrandizing segregation.

Chapter 7: Mirror Mirror on the Wall, will the Judiciary save us all?

The Indian Constitution, which is federal in nature, establishes a separation of powers between the legislature, the executive, and the judiciary. These powers, however, are not absolute and are only subject to check in the sense of their own constitution. As a global institution, the judiciary aspired to be the defender and protector of human rights.

According to the Indian Constitution, the superior judiciary, which includes the Supreme Court of India and the High Courts, is responsible for this role. When it comes to the defence of human rights, the Supreme Court of India is one of the most successful courts in the country. The judiciary's independence is one of the fundamental features of the Indian constitution. Legislation is made by states, but due to a fundamental provision of the constitution, it is still subject to judicial review. The Indian legislature has passed many laws regarding the rights of prisoners in jail, but because they are a venerable class, they are continually abused. Despite the clauses of our constitution and other constitutional legislation protecting prisoners' rights, they remain an abused and venerable class of society. The Supreme Court of India has spoken about this issue and laid down different guidelines to secure the rights of this earthen class on many occasions through various judgments, demonstrating that despite all laws and provisions, the implication at ground zero is flawed and needs investigation. The researcher's goal would be to find these ground realities, evaluate the Supreme Court's guidelines, and come up with some solutions to the problem through doctrinal analysis.

The Supreme Court has held that the provisions of Part III of the Constitution should be given the broadest possible meaning in the following cases: Maneka Gandhi, Sunil Batra (I), M.H.Hoskot, and Hussainara Khatoon.

Though not specifically stated, it has been held that the right to legal aid, a speedy trial, the right to have an interview with a friend, relative, or lawyer, the protection of prisoners in jail from degrading, inhumane, and barbarous treatment, the right to travel abroad, the right to live with human dignity, and the right to livelihood, among other things, are Fundamental Rights under Article 21 of the Constitution[181]. As a result, the Supreme Court of India has significantly expanded the reach of Article 21 and declared that it would

---

[181] 1978 SCR (2) 621

be available for protecting prisoners' constitutional rights and enacting prison reforms. The Supreme Court of India has developed Human Rights jurisprudence to preserve and protect the Right to Human Dignity of prisoners[182]. The Apex judiciary's concern can be seen in the numerous cardinal judicial decisions. The Supreme Court's ruling in Sunil Batra was a landmark moment in India's prison jurisprudence.

Prison is an integral part of the criminal justice system where inmates are stripped of their liberty for the intent of reformation[183]. So it's a prison or a place where they're incarcerated (for the purpose of reformation). As a result, prisons are factories where criminals are produced on a daily basis as a result of state crime. In India, prisons are regarded as a key source of human

---

[182] 1980 AIR 1579
[183] Singh, S., *"Role of the Supreme Court towards a New Prison Jurisprudence"*, 6 Student Adv. (1994).

rights abuses. As an inmate, they have protections against problems like inadequate housing, unsanitary conditions, indiscriminate huddling of inmates, mental and physical torture, lack of legal representation, inadequate bedding facilities, and insufficient medical facilities, among others. The Universal Declaration of Human Rights played a significant role in recognising the different rights of prisoners. So, by the late 1970s, the pattern of treating prisoners as outcasts had reversed, and with the aid of UDHRs, the trend of treating them as human beings had begun.

The Antiquated and Colonial Prison Act of 1894 governs India's jails, which treats inmates as the state's slaves. This act calls for punitive and deterrent punishments. As a result, it is an out-of-date act that is now in conflict with legal norms as well as culture, necessitating certain changes because society is complex in nature.

As a result, the role of the judiciary in protecting the rights of prisoners is vital, as it is the guardian of those rights.

In the last decade, there has been a growing awareness of the importance of prison reforms, and it is now widely accepted that a reformative ideology and a rehabilitative approach are required components of prison justice. As a result, India's current prison administration is a legacy of British rule. It is founded on the premise that even the strongest criminal code would be of no benefit to a society unless there is efficient punishment machinery in place. The Second Commission of Inquiry into Jail Management and Discipline, formed in 1864, made similar recommendations to the 1836 Committee. There has been an increasing understanding of the value of prison reforms over the last decade, and it is now generally recognised that a reformative philosophy and a rehabilitative approach are necessary components of prison justice. As a consequence, the new Indian prison system is a legacy of British rule. It is based on the principle that even the strictest criminal code will be meaningless to a society unless it is followed by successful punishment mechanisms. Similar recommendations were made to the 1836 Committee by the Second Commission of Inquiry into Jail Management and Discipline, which was established in 1864.

Prisons in India are regulated by the antiquated and colonial Prison Act of 1894, which promotes retributive and deterrent forms of punishment and considers prisoners to be "slaves of the state." Prisoners are subjected to inhumane treatment, torture, and handcuffing, which is in several ways in violation of Art. 21. Their personal lives and liberties are taken away from them, and public authorities are inhuman to the inmates. Prisoners are still human beings, and their dignity cannot be taken away from them. However, the truth is different, despite the fact that some laws pertaining to prisoners' rights are not properly enforced. In addition, prisoners are denied basic rights such as access to bedding, medical care, food, and clothes, as well as living in an unsanitary environment.

There are numerous provisions in various acts to protect the rights of prisoners, but the judiciary has played a significant role in protecting the rights of prisoners by issuing such judgments and guidelines. The judiciary has interpreted various provisions of the constitution to provide an overview of prisoners' rights. However, in fact, all of these provisions are not being fully enforced. Prisoners have to suffer or have their freedom stripped away from them. There are many explanations for this, including the lack of a deterrence impact on stakeholders and the failure to enforce the provisions.

The Indian constitution and other procedural laws include several provisions and laws prohibiting violations of prisoners' rights. Although such rights are not explicitly specified in the constitution, the Supreme Court has played an important role in interpreting Articles 14, 19, and 21 in Part 3 as well as Articles 39A, 42, 39, and 38 in Part 4 to provide or spell out various fundamental rights to prisoners. Articles 14 and 19 of the constitution can be used to interpret terms like torture and cruel punishment. Often the third degree is applied, which is in violation of Article 21 of the constitution, which protects human dignity. There is no point in having such rights if there is no way to enforce them. Article 32 of the Indian constitution provides for writs such as habeas corpus, mandamus, quo warranto, prohibition, and certiorari. A individual may sue the supreme court directly for a violation of such rights, or the high court under article 226 for a violation of such rights. As an independent judiciary, the Supreme Court is the protector of such rights, and it has established some rules that run parallel to such rights. It also keeps an eye on the lagislautre to ensure that no new laws infringe on such rights are passed, as they are subject to judicial review. According to this view, prisoners have certain human rights, which they cannot be denied, but they may be stripped of their liberty to some extent for the purpose of reformation.

As a result, prisoners have rights that cannot be taken away from them. Although these rights are guaranteed by the constitution, they are not absolute, and certain limitations are placed on them, such as the right to personal liberty, which is one of the most essential among fundamental rights. When a person is arrested and sentenced to jail, he no longer has the status of a regular person.

Prisoners are people, too, and they should be handled as such. As a result, inmates have a right to be free from inhumane treatment by various officials, such as the jail authorities and police officers. When inmates are tortured or subjected to inhumane treatment in police custody, the concerned authority has violated Articles 14 and 19 of the constitution. Similarly, third-degree assault by the police is a violation of article 21, i.e. human dignity. In Raghubir Singh v. State of Bihar[184], the supreme court expressed its displeasure with police torture by upholding a life sentence granted to a police officer who was

---

[184] 1987 AIR 149

responsible for the death of a suspect as a result of torture in a police holding cell[185]. The Supreme Court ruled in Kishore Singh v. State of Rajasthan[186] that the use of third-degree methods by police is a violation of Article 21 and that the law does not allow the use of third-degree methods or torture on an accused person because "state actions must be right, just, and fair, torture for extracting some kind of confession will neither be right nor fair".

Solitary confinement and Bar Fetters are against the spirit of the constitution, and such punishments reduce the prisoner to an animal. As a result, such a sentence is considered cruel and unusual, as it subjected the inmate to mental torment. As a result, inmates have a right to be free of solitary confinement

[185] Upadhyay, Minal H., *"Role of Judiciary ib Protecting the Human Rights of Prisoners"*, IJRHSS Vol. 2, Issue 8 (2014)
[186] 1981 AIR 625

and shackles. In addition, Indian courts have repeatedly held that such a sentence has a degrading and dehumanising effect on the inmates. The Supreme Court debated the legality of solitary confinement in the Sunil Batra case[187]. It should only be enforced under rare circumstances, such as when a convicted offender is of such a violent nature or character that he needs to be isolated from other inmates. If we examine solitary confinement and shackles in the context of the constitution, we will find that they are unlawful actions taken against the prisoner, infringing on the fundamental right to life and personal liberty. It is undeniable that prisoners have some human rights that are more limited than those of the general public, but this does not exclude them from being stripped of them by such punishment.

---

[187] Sunil Batra (I) vs. Delhi Administration. AIR 1978 SC 1675

Since our justice system uses a reformative rather than a retributive approach to punishment, such extreme and inhuman punishment can only be viewed as a breach of the constitution.

The basic goal of any judicial system in a democratic state is to provide people with a fair and speedy trial. The right to a speedy trial is now a widely acknowledged human right. As an autonomous judiciary, it is the judiciary's obligation to grant certain privileges. As a custodian of rights, the constitution guarantees suspects, offenders, and inmates the right to a speedy trial. If a court fails to grant this right, the phrase "justice deferred is justice denied" applies. The accused has suffered a great deal as a result of the excessive or incompetent trial or prosecution delay. A person who has been convicted has the right to a speedy trial and he has the right to appeal his conviction. Under section 309 of the Code of Criminal Procedure, there is a provision for the procedure of investigation and prosecution of an offence with respect to speedy trial. There will be no definition of delayed justice if such a clause is followed in a reasonable way, but it will not be properly enforced in its original spirit. As a result, in A. R. Antulay v. R. S. Nayak[188], the Supreme Court developed the following principles, which would go a long way in protecting the Human Rights of prisoners. The right to a speedy trial is also derived from Article 21 of the Indian constitution, according to the apex court. A prisoner's right to appeal, revision, and revisit his sentence cannot be taken away from him while he is incarcerated. If a court takes an unreasonable, unexplained, unjust, or negligently long time to pronounce a judgment, it would be deemed a

---

[188] 1988 AIR 1531

breach of Article 21 of the Indian constitution. After reading Articles 21 and 39-A, as well as Article 142 and Section 304 of the Cr.PC, a three-judge bench of the Supreme Court (V.R.Krishna Iyer, D.A.Desai, and O.Chinnappa Reddy, JJ[189]) ruled that the government has a responsibility to provide legal services to the accused[190]. The 42nd Constitution Amendment Act of 1976 added Article 39A to the constitution as a free legal aid clause. This is the most relevant clause in the Indian constitution, which provides free legal assistance. Since it was inserted under the State Policy Directive Principles, this article is not enforceable. This is one of the directives to state policy in state government. Parliament has passed the Legal Service Authorities Act 1987, which guarantees free legal services, and other states formed Legal Aid and Advice Boards. This

---

[189] 1978 AIR 1548
[190] Nair, S., *"Prison Justice and the Court"*, (1978) CULR 336

free legal assistance is not limited to criminal cases; it is also available in civil, tax, and administrative matters. With the passing of time, the Human Right's horizon continues to grow. Prisoners' rights do not only apply to physical abuse; they also apply to mental torture. Article 21 of the constitution guarantees the right to life and personal liberty. It can be deduced from this that an inmate has the right to meet with or have an interview with his family, friends, and law enforcement officers. Since, according to article 21, a prisoner has the right to personal liberty, including the right to see his family and friends, and article 22(1) expressly states that an imprisoned person cannot be refused the right to consult and be represented by a lawyer of his choosing. This legal right is also secured by section 304 of the Code of Criminal Procedure. In addition, the interests of inmates are regularly covered by court decisions. In Dharambir v. State of Uttar Pradesh[191], the court ordered the State Government to allow family members to meet the prisoners and for the prisoners to visit their families at least once a year, under controlled conditions. In other cases, the court has held that an interview with the inmate is needed for accurate information. The Supreme Court ruled in another landmark case, Francis Coralie Mullin v. The Administrator, Union Territory of Delhi & others[192], that a detainee's right to life and liberty included his right to live with dignity, and that a detainee must be allowed to have interviews with relatives, friends, and lawyers without extreme restrictions.

The right to be handcuffed is one of the most valuable rights that an inmate or convicted person has. It is considered more harsh, inhumane,

---

[191] 1979 AIR 1595
[192] 1981 AIR 746

and arbitrary in nature because it affects human dignity. The right to freedom is guaranteed by Article 19 of the Indian constitution, but this type of arbitrary action is a violation of that right. Both the accused and the inmate have a right to be free of handcuffs (in the judicial custody and trial in process). In special situations where police officers have reason to believe that a suspect or inmate may be absconding, hand cuffing may be required.

Binding a man hand and foot with steel shuffle hoops, taking him to court in such a state, and standing him in the court for hours is mental torment for him. This form of torture is dehumanizing since it sometimes lasts longer than the suspected offence penalty. The Supreme Court also claimed that it should not be done on a daily basis because it violates human dignity. For him, it is a kind of mental torture. However, police officers do not obey these rules, and inmates suffer as a result.

As for the different rights that are given to prisoners, as discussed above, a liberal perspective has been adopted to demonstrate the rights of prisoners that are in compliance with humanitarian grounds. These protections should be given to inmates not because they are criminals or offenders, but because they are still humans.

In India, prisons and their administration fall under the State List since they are a state subject protected by item 4 of the State List in the Indian constitution's Seventh Schedule. State governments are responsible for the supervision and administration of jails, which are regulated by the Prison Act of 1894. States have the authority and duty to update and modernize prison laws, guidelines, and regulations that are obsolete and incompatible with society. The Central Government assists in various aspects of the prison system, including defence, medical services, and the repair and reconstruction of old prisons. The government also works to develop borstal schools, women offenders' services, and other reformation training.

The judiciary has also shown its significance in various areas of prison administration. The Supreme Court of India has established three general principles in relation to the prison status as well as the status of prisoners in jail, which are used as guidelines by the higher judiciary. To begin with, a prisoner does not become anonymous. Second, a person in prison is entitled to all human rights within the confines of his or her confinement. Finally, there is no excuse for exacerbating the misery already present in the prison phase.

Convicts, under-trials, and Detenues are the three types of prisoners in India's prisons. A prisoner is someone who has been found guilty of a crime and has been convicted by the judge. An individual who is currently on trial in a court of law is known as an under trial. A detune is someone who is being held in judicial custody. Civil prisoners are those that are incarcerated for offences that do not fall under the Indian Penal Code. Civil detainees are only those who have been convicted or are awaiting trial.

Prisoners' living conditions are deplorable, and they are handled as if they were livestock. The lack of basic facilities on the prison grounds makes it difficult to stay alive while incarcerated. They don't have access to even the most basic necessities for life. The food given to them is of low quality and unfit for consumption. They are also sexually abused by both the jail authorities and their fellow inmates. Their grievances have remained unresolved. They are subjected to harsh abuse by the hardcore offenders who possess the bulk of power in the prison. They are exposed to long working hours without obtaining any compensation. In jail, life is nothing short of hell. This question has been raised many times, but the parliament has yet to adequately discuss it. The overcrowding in the prison, which literally means overcapacity, is also a significant problem. The lack of sensitivity on the part of the courts and the legislature should be remedied as soon as possible. They must remember that inmates have the same rights as anyone else, including the right to life and the right to pursue justice. If the interests of inmates are not addressed, the dignity element and the justice principle enshrined in the preamble will be defeated.

In regards to my study, it demonstrates that the number of prisons in India is comparatively low in comparison to the number of inmates who are brought into the prisons, as the figures are increasing day by day due to a rise in the number of illegal activities in society and the judiciary's inability to resolve cases. As a result, my recommendation is that the government work against this goal by increasing the number of prisons and improving the conditions of the inmates and the services available to them in the prisons.

More than a decade has passed since 1894, but the only legislative policy void is that there is no legislation relating to the rights of prisoners. The formulation of a national policy on prisons and prisoners was recommended by the Mulla committee on jail reform. After that, several attempts were made, including the government drafting a new bill with the support of the NHRC (NATIONAL HUMAN RIGHTS COMMISSION), but the hope of seeing it passed in parliament has remained unfulfilled to this day. Due to the legislature's inaction in the area of enacting laws for prisoners, the judiciary was forced to step into the position of policymaker and play a proactive role in providing natural human rights to this previously unrecognised group of people. While the constitution protects human rights, there are no clear provisions for prisoners' rights. However, the judiciary played an important role in interpreting those rights based on various constitutional provisions. It is the legislature's obligation to pass legislation in various areas, but the legislature has declined to do so in the area of prisoners' rights.

Part III of the constitution guarantees citizens' human rights, and inmates are considered citizens as well, so they have these rights as well, though they are subject to more restrictions than the average individual. The majority of rights are understood from Part III of the constitution, although they are not explicitly stated. India is one of the world's largest democratic nations, with a function of separation of powers that enables the legislature to pass particular laws and amendments. Since we have a Parliamentary form of government with a federal structure, the legislative enacting system has become more difficult. The legislature must follow a clear protocol when enacting legislation. There are several parties in India, and the same is true in the parliament, making the process more complicated. Many opposition parties oppose the law by misinterpreting it, causing the legislative process to become more complicated. As a result of the inability of legislation to pass laws in respect of prisoners' rights, there are no checks and balances in place in the prison to ensure that the jail authority operates properly. However, as a protector of rights, the Supreme Court has developed several rules for prisons and prisoners' rights, but they are not followed in practise. In various cases, India's Supreme Court has issued guidelines for the safety of prisoners' rights. We recognise that prisoners are lawbreakers and a threat to society because of the legislative void, but jail is an institution for the reformation of such lawbreakers. As a result, it is the legislature's responsibility to enact legislation that is most conducive to change. There is a Prison Act of 1894, which was amended after January 1, 1957, but it is insufficient to protect the rights of prisoners. Since it is devoid of clauses pertaining to prisoners' rights.

The rules that regulate India's prisons date back to 1864, and the statute, which was drafted by the British, is still in use by the Indian government today. This is the main shortcoming of the parliament, which has passed a number of new laws and changes to existing laws but has yet to enact any amendments or new laws relating to the rights of prisoners. So, my suggestion is that the parliament should work seriously on this issue and draught new laws concerning the rights of prisoners, as this is a demand of modern society today. Given that India is in the midst of a period of smart governance, how can the parliament continue to follow the old law, which was enacted by the British in the year 1864?

Every country's judiciary has a duty and a constitutional function to protect citizens' human rights. This role is allocated to the superior judiciary, namely the Supreme Court of India and the High Courts, by the Constitution of India. The Supreme Court of India is one of the most successful courts in the world when it comes to human rights security. It has a strong reputation for independence and trustworthiness. The division of powers, in which the executive, legislature, and judiciary constitute three branches of government, is the basis of the autonomous judicial system. The judiciary's effectiveness in upholding the rule of law and human rights is dependent on this separation and consequent independence.

Since every state has a judicial system to protect its law-abiding citizens, it must also have jails for those who break the law. However, this does not imply that the detainees have no rights. Prisoners have their own collection of protections. The Supreme Court of India has established human rights jurisprudence for the preservation and protection of prisoners' rights to preserve human dignity by reading Article 21 of the Constitution. Any violation of this right is punishable under Article 14 of the Constitution, which guarantees equality and equal treatment under the law. In addition, the Prison Act of 1894 and the Criminal Procedure Code address the issue of prisoner brutality (CRPC). Any violation of a prisoner's rights by police officers draws the attention of both the legislature and the judiciary. In recent years, the Indian judiciary, especially the Supreme Court, has been extremely vigilant against violations of prisoners' human rights. The Supreme Court and the High Courts have also expressed their displeasure with the prison conditions, which have resulted in violations of prisoners' rights. The interests of prisoners have become a hot subject in prison reform debates.

During the last three or four decades, the need for prison reform has become more evident.

In recent years, the Supreme Court of India has been particularly proactive in its enforcement of prisoners' human rights. "No person shall be deprived of his life or personal liberty except in accordance with the procedure provided by law," according to Article 21 of the Indian Constitution. Human Rights in India are built on the rights to life and personal liberty. The Indian judiciary has acted as an institution for providing successful redress against abuses of Human Rights through its constructive approach and activism. The courts have formulated and defined a multitude of rights by giving "life and personal liberty" a liberal and detailed interpretation. The Fundamental Rights enshrined in Article 21 were granted a rather narrow and concrete reading by the court. The court in A. K. Gopalan's case[193] held that each Article dealt with distinct rights that had no connection to one another, i.e. they were mutually exclusive. However, in the Maneka Gandhi case[194], it was held that they are not mutually exclusive, but rather form a single scheme in the Constitution, and that they are all parts of an integrated scheme. "The ambit of Personal Liberty as established by Article 21 of the Constitution is broad and comprehensive," the court stated in this case. It includes both substantive rights to personal liberty and the legal procedures for deprivation of those rights," he added, adding that the legal procedures must be equal, just, and rational.

The Supreme Court has held that the provisions of Part III should be given the broadest possible meaning in the following cases: Maneka Gandhi,

---

[193] 1950 AIR 27
[194] 1978 AIR 597

Sunil Batra (I), M.H.Hoskot, and Hussainara Khatoon. Though not expressly stated, it has been held that the right to legal aid, a speedy trial, the right to have an interview with a friend, relative, or lawyer, the security of prisoners in jail from degrading, inhumane, and barbarous treatment, the right to travel abroad, the right to live with dignity, and the right to livelihood are all Fundamental Rights under Article 21 of the Constitution. As a result, the Supreme Court of India has significantly expanded the reach of Article 21 and declared that it would be available for protecting prisoners' constitutional rights and enacting prison reforms. The Indian Supreme Court has developed Human Rights jurisprudence to preserve and protect the Right to Human Dignity of prisoners. The Apex judiciary's concern can be seen in the numerous cardinal judicial decisions. The Supreme Court's decision in Sunil

Batra[195] was a turning point in the history of Indian prison law.

The courts have taken a clear stance against solitary confinement, ruling that it has a highly punishing and dehumanising impact on the prisoners. The courts have ruled that it should only be enforced under extreme situations, such as when the prisoner is so violent that he has to be isolated from the other inmates. In Sunil Batra (1)[196], the Supreme Court found the legality of solitary confinement. The Supreme Court has also expressed strong opposition to the imposition of bar fetters on the inmates. The court stated that holding a prisoner in fetters 24 hours a day, 7 days a week reduced the prisoner to an animal, and that such treatment was so cruel and unusual that the use of bar fetters was against the spirit of the Indian Constitution.

---

[195] 1980 AIR 1579
[196] 1979 SCR (1) 392

Human Dignity is inextricably linked to Human Rights. In a number of occasions, the Supreme Court of India has taken serious notice of inhumane treatment of prisoners and has given effective directions to prison and police authorities to protect the rights of prisoners and people in police custody. The Supreme Court interpreted Articles 14 and 19 of the Constitution to provide a right against torture. "The treatment of a human being that offends human dignity, imposes avoidable torture, and reduces the man to the level of a beast will definitely be arbitrary and can be called into question under Article 14," the court said. In Raghubir Singh v. State of Bihar, the Supreme Court expressed its displeasure with police torture by upholding a life sentence granted to a police officer who was responsible for the death of a suspect as a result of torture in a police detention facility.

The Supreme Court ruled in Kishore Singh vs. State of Rajasthan that police use of the third degree procedure is a breach of Article 21. The Supreme Court's decision in the case of D.K. Basu is noteworthy. While hearing the case, the court centred on the question of incarceration torture and released a range of guidelines aimed at eradicating this heinous crime and strengthening the security and promotion of human rights. The Supreme Court established torture and considered its ramifications in this case.

Human Rights is broadening its horizons. Prisoners' rights have been recognised to protect them not only from physical pain or torture in person, but also from mental torture. Article 21's right to life and personal liberty cannot be limited to the nature of animals. It implies a lot more than just physical survival. The right to have an interview with members of one's family and friends is explicitly part of Article 21's Personal Liberty. Article 22 (I) of the Constitution states that no one who has been arrested is denied the right to meet with and be represented by a lawyer of his choosing. Section 30441 of the Code of Criminal Procedure also provides for this legal right. This right accrues to the accused person from the moment of detention, according to the court, and he has the right to select his own lawyer. The Supreme Court of India found the extent of a prisoner's or detainee's right to have interviews with family members, colleagues, and counsel in a series of cases. In Dharmbir vs. State of Uttar Pradesh[197], the court ordered the state government to allow family members to meet the prisoners and to allow the prisoners to visit their

---

[197] 1979 AIR 1595

families under guarded conditions at least once a year.

The Supreme Court held in Hussainara Khatoon vs. Home Secretary, Bihar[198], that any accused person who is unable to hire a lawyer and obtain legal services due to reasons such as poverty, indigence, or incommunicado status has a constitutional right to have free legal services given to him by the state, and that the state has a constitutional obligation to provide such a lawyer. If no free legal services are given, the trial may be void as a violation of Article 21.

The court held in Sheela Barse vs. State of Maharashtra[199] that prisoner interviews are required because otherwise accurate information can not be obtained, but that such access must be monitored and regulated. The court stated in Jogindar Kumar vs. State of Uttar Pradesh[200] that the

---

[198] 1979 SCR (3) 532
[199] JT 1988 (3) 15

horizon of Human Rights is widening as the crime rate is also rising, and that the court has been receiving complaints about Human Rights violations due to indiscriminate arrests. The court stated that everyone has the right to be educated. One of the primary goals of the criminal justice system is for offences to be tried as quickly as possible. When the court has taken cognizance of the charge, the trial must proceed swiftly in order to convict the guilty and absolve the innocent. Unless the accused is proven, everyone is presumed innocent. As a result, the accused's quality or innocence must be assessed as soon as possible. As a consequence, it is the court's responsibility to ensure that no convicted party avoids justice, and it is also the court's responsibility to ensure that the accused persons are not harassed indefinitely. It is important to note that "delay in trial by itself constitutes denial of justice," as "justice delayed is justice denied" is said. It is important that those convicted of crimes be prosecuted quickly so that, in the event that bail is rejected, the accused may not have to spend more time in prison than is absolutely required. The right to a speedy trial is now regarded as a fundamental human right.

The code of criminal procedure contains the primary procedure for investigating and prosecuting an offence with respect to speedy trial.

The right to a speedy trial is covered by section 309 of the Criminal Procedure Code. There would be no cause for complaint if the terms of the Cr.PC were followed to the letter and intent. However, these laws are not being carried out in their spirit. The constitutional guarantee of a speedy trial, as enshrined in Article 21, must be properly reflected in the provisions of the code. The Supreme Court has laid down the following propositions in A. R. Antulay vs. R. S. Nayak for this reason, which would go a long way in securing the Human Rights of prisoners. The Supreme Court ruled in this case that the right to a speedy trial guaranteed by Article 21 of the Constitution applies to accused at all stages of the process, including investigation, inquiry, trial, appeal, review, and retrial.

Despite the fact that the Indian Constitution does not explicitly provide for the right to legal assistance, the judiciary has favoured poor prisoners who are unable to afford a lawyer of their choosing due to their poverty. Under Article 39A of the Constitution, the 42nd Amendment Act of 1976 provided Free Legal Assistance as one of the Directive Principles of State Policy. Free Legal Aid is included in the Constitution's most relevant and direct article. Despite the fact that this Article is found in Part IV of the Constitution as one of the Directive Principles of State Policy, and despite the fact that it is not enforceable by courts, the principles set out in it are critical to the country's governance. The state is bound by Article 37 of the Constitution to apply these principles when making laws. Article 38, on the other hand, imposes an obligation on the state to promote the welfare of the people by securing and protecting as effectively as possible a constitutional order in which social, economic, and political justice inform all aspects of national life. To give effect to the Constitutional mandate of Article 39-A, the parliament enacted the Legal Services Authorities Act, 1987, which guarantees legal aid, and various state governments formed legal aid and advice boards and framed schemes for free legal aid and incidental matters. Legal Help is more commonly available under Indian Human Rights law, and it is available not only in criminal cases, but also in civil, revenue, and administrative cases.

In Madhav Hayawadan Rao Hoskot vs. State of Maharashtra[201], a three-judge bench of the Supreme Court (V.R.Krishna Iyer, D.A.Desai, and O.Chinnappa Reddy, JJ) read Articles 21 and 39-A, as well as Article 142 and section 304 of the Cr.PC, and concluded that the government had a responsibility to provide legal services to the accused.

The Supreme Court added another projectile to its arsenal in Prem Shanker vs. Delhi Government[202], which would be used against the war on prison reform and prisoner rights. The issue in this case was whether or not handcuffing is legally permissible. The Supreme Court went through the handcuffing jurisprudence in great

[201] 1978 AIR 1548
[202] 1980 AIR 1535

detail. It is the argument that has been brought before the court as a Public Interest Litigation, requesting that the court rule on the constitutional validity of the "hand cuffing culture" in light of Article 21 of the Constitution. In this case, the court declared the distinction between groups of prisoners to be obsolete and declared compulsory handcuffing of prisoners to be a Constitutional mandate. The court also stated that "hand cuffing is prima-facie inhuman and, therefore, unfair," and that it is "overly harsh and, at first blush, arbitrary." To inflict "irons" in the absence of a reasonable procedure and impartial control is to resort to zoological techniques, which are in violation of Article 21 of the Constitution."

The Supreme Court ruled in Selvi vs State of Karnataka[203] that narco - analysis, polygraph testing, and brain

---

[203] AIR 2010 SC 1974

mapping are illegal and violate human rights. This decision is unfavourable to multiple investigating agencies because it would obstruct the progress of investigations, and many convicted suspects will be able to avoid prosecution as a result of this new role. However, the Supreme Court went on to say that such tests can only be carried out if an individual consents to them. The results of the tests will not be admissible in court as evidence, but will only be used to further the investigation. With advancements in technology and neurology, Narcoanalysis, Polygraph testing, and Brain Mapping have become popular techniques utilised by law enforcement agencies across the world to extract the truth from suspects. However, dissenting voices will finally be heard. They were characterised as a crime against humanity and a violation of an individual's right to privacy.

The Supreme Court agreed that the assessments in question are in violation of Article 20 (3) of the Constitution, which states that no one may be compelled to testify against himself. The court also told the investigating agencies that the National Human Rights Commission's directives should be strictly followed when performing the examinations. These tests have previously been used in a variety of cases, including the Arushi Talwar murder case, the Nithari killings case, the Abdul Telagi case, the Abu Salem case, the Pragya Thakur (Bomb blast case), and others.

To sum up, a study of the Indian judiciary's decisions concerning the defence of prisoners' human rights reveals that the judiciary has acted as a saviour in circumstances where the executive and legislature have struggled to solve the people's problems. The Supreme Court has stepped in to take corrective action to give the executive and legislative branches the guidance they need. After reading the above contribution, it is clear that the Indian judiciary has been very sensitive to and aware of the security of people's human rights.

Chapter 8: Handcuffs weigh much more than Gravestones.

An Albanian poet named Visar Zhiti said "Handcuffs weigh much more than Gravestones"[204] and its true for many people in India as well who suffer prison time. This is so because when a person goes to gravestone he is dead and there's nothing left behind but it is so that when a person comes out of prison he is dead but he is left behind to drag himself round the clock for the number of days he lives from that period. There is not much a person can do after returning from prison because the number of restrictions put on that person from the State, the general outcasting by the society which all leads up to a person returned from prison facing huge difficulty in re-establishing his life. No matter what, once a person

---

[204] Visar Zhiti, Robert Elsa, "*The Condemned Apple: Selected Poetry*", Green Integer; Bilingual Edition (1 May 2004)

has been convicted of an offence and is sent to prison sentence and is now released after completing the prison sentence yet the attitude towards the person of people knowing of the antecedent still remains the same as it was to be towards a person convicted of an offence, then what good did the prison sentence do if the people around still treat the person as a person convicted of the offence.

The label of a criminal never goes, even sitting Members of Parliaments are hurled as criminals sometimes despite being clear of charges against them, merely because once some sort of charges were levied against them. What is the responsibility of the state in such a scenario? And we call out the state to take responsibility because it is the policy maker, it is the law – enforcer and basically sets the direction in which a society moves. Now, if every second person in the society will live in the fear of going to prison then (s)he shall continue to do illegal wrongful activities but his sole ambition shall be not to get caught. He shall fear his fellow citizens that maybe someone would file a complaint against them for an offence they never committed and put them behind bars, maybe temporarily only but still the fear of experiencing prison time will be there. It should be the responsibility of the state that every prisoner be provided with a legal counsel if he cannot afford one for himself immediately upon arrest. The Government should set examples by punishing police officers and also his team if the person arrested is physically harmed in the process of interrogation. Every person deserves to be treated like a human and the rules exist in writing but very little seems to be happening on those lines in this Country. We have made laws for humane treatment but we have failed to implement them in our prison system, and that is because the prison officials aren't well trained and sensitized enough to follow it. Rather, they sometimes in the company of criminals start acting in the similar fashion themselves and if you ask them they would say that its only hits and sticks that these prisoners "deserve" and that they are being lenient by giving them food, the food of the quality that they wouldn't even have on their worst day. The prison officials in this country act in the similar fashion as if they are still a Victorian Employee employed to maintain law and order in the Indian Subcontinent. They assume themselves to belong to a different elitist kind of class of people when compared to prison inmates and this kind of mindset is what causes harm to prison inmates. When the prison authorities think of prison inmates as some kind of low-life person then they try to assert their whims and fancies upon them. There are records of female inmates complaining about prison staff misbehaving with them, of prison officers taking sexual favours in the name of letting them free of jail, etc. These are inhuman and animal like behaviour which the prison administration people are indulging in and it is expected that they should know this better.

The judiciary is there to complain about the violations of laws and rules formulated by the legislature but the State has forgotten the part where it bridges the gap in between these two, i.e., how to complain to the judiciary about the violations of rules and laws made by the legislature? How does a prisoner complaint about the prison administration? There is a rule that suggests that Hon'ble Sessions Judge's to visit prisons every week and there are such other rules but what does the Hon'ble Sessions Judge do upon his visit? The absence of details leaves the prisoners at the mercy of NGO volunteers' occasional visits to the prison to hear out their concerns and if one is lucky then maybe his case is taken up by the NGO and they fight on his behalf. Now, we understand when the head of the State says the Government has no business in doing business but to protect its citizen is its principle task, it is why we have an elected form of government, to protect the interests of the citizen. For this gap to be bridged, like every High Court has an Advocate General and accompanying Additional Advocate General's appointed to represent the State for which they are appointed and their office is compensated as the cases are taken up respectively, similarly a Senior Advocate must be appointed in every District & Sessions Court and in High Court of every state whose role shall be to take up cases of people in prison who are not able to afford a legal counsel for themselves. We need to address fundamental issues regarding problems in the prison system and overpopulation is one of it.

To begin with, the idea that one must be punished for whatever wrong he has done must be eradicated from the minds of the people. It should be shifted towards making people more humane. The primary task should be eradicating the punitive system with a reformative system and reformation should not be through inflicting pain and torture on the human. A person when realized about his mistakes can always transform himself in a good citizen of the society if he is provided with the right environment. So long as it remains a punitive center, the stigma attached with it shall continue and hence will leave with a very small scope for people coming out of these centers for reintegration in their old societies. But this is something that the State should adopt.

Meanwhile, in the current scenario there is also a huge scope of helping the prisoners if one wishes to! Every law college has an established legal aid cell with law students and professors as its members and there are various lawyers organizations having a legal aid cell too. But to limit them with if someone approaches them concept the real idea of legal aid cell shall not thrive. To use this platform the members should engage in prison visits and offer them their support and engage in fighting for their legal rights and battles. As mentioned previously there are people imprisoned in prisons for period much more than the maximum prison period for the offence they have been accused / convicted with but because they are unaware of the law, or they have no resources to hire a lawyer or are not in a position to bribe for government legal aid get stuck in prisons forever and this can be stopped by taking a small step that every weekend the members of legal aid cells go to prisons and talk to the prisoners and if they find somewhere someone's rights have been infringed, they must bring this to their in-charges and take up the legal fight for these prisoners. This shall be a great learning experience too for the law students, a real client counseling and drafting and maybe even trial experience as against that fancy moot-court experience. The platform already exists, whether it is to tick a box for affiliation purposes or to actually meet a purpose is in the hands of the institution and the members of the cell.

So long as the state believes in punishing and not reforming we can not even talk about rehabilitating the prisoners whereas the only right way to reduce crime in a society is to create good citizens, and good citizens in an independent democratic country can not be with a regressive punitive criminal justice system. The State needs to shift its focus to having more educated class of citizen who have the basic ability to reason between what is right and wrong. If a person lacks the ability to differentiate between right and wrong, it is always possible he might end up doing something wrong. Then when he is convicted of the wrongdoing, in the current system he shall be punished for the wrong he has committed and when released maybe with fear he may never commit that wrong again but still he does not has the ability to reason between what is right and what is wrong because he has only been punished not reformed and absolutely not rehabilitated and hence maybe due to fear he won't commit that wrong but he might end up committing another wrong and hence we should ask what good did it do? What was the return of all the public tax money spent on him during his time at prison if he still comes out to be the same person that he was before entering the system.

The recidivism factor must be the fundamental point to address while reforming the prison system and the criminal law of the country. The State needs to scrap this nearly 2 century old law with something that works for a now independent country as the law that governs us today was established to maintain peace in a colonial rule and not an independent society. If a system fails to reduce recidivism then it is not working and is a waste of public money. The focus should be to reform and rehabilitate wrongdoers into fit citizens for the society, and only that would mean true win for a prison system, only then every Sinner will have a future!

www.ingramcontent.com/pod-product-compliance
Lightning Source LLC
Chambersburg PA
CBHW070325220526
45467CB00001B/32